To Gladis,
at 6:15 P.M.
June 11, 1941.
From

Stanley

ANYONE CAN DRAW!

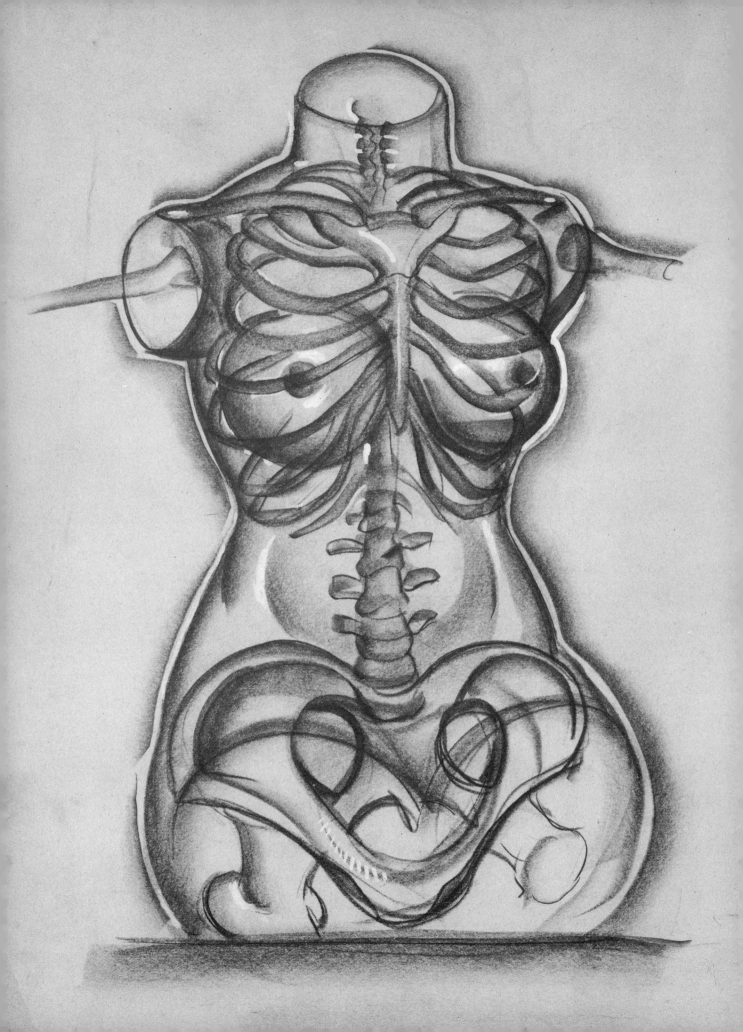

Anyone Can Draw!

BY ARTHUR ZAIDENBERG

INSTRUCTOR IN DRAWING, NEW YORK UNIVERSITY

MEMBER OF FACULTY, ROERICH ACADEMY OF ARTS

Text in collaboration with Jerome Darwin Engel

A complete, practical course in art instruction. With an introduction by JOSEPH TCHAKIN, Guest Lecturer on Art, Oxford and Sorbonne Universities, and critical commentary by GEORGE GOMBARTS, Principal, School of Industrial Design, Board of Education, New York

ILLUSTRATED EDITIONS COMPANY, INC.
220 FOURTH AVENUE   NEW YORK
1940

Contents

TO CLARA

The publishers wish to express their appreciation to those who have materially assisted in this work.

They are particularly indebted to Joseph M. Mann, who supervised the production of this book, for his thoroughness and for his many valued recommendations.

They also wish to thank Louis Klepper, Bernard Halpern, R. L. Weiner and Monte J Sacks for helpful advice and criticism.

* * *

All illustrations in this volume—with the exception of those by the great masters in the Gallery, pages 309 to 360, and those on page 259—are the work of the author, Arthur Zaidenberg.

Introduction

BY JOSEPH TCHAKIN

GUEST LECTURER ON ART, OXFORD
AND SORBONNE UNIVERSITIES

When the child laboriously traces the crude outlines of the engine he would like to have, or the toy truck he saw in a store window, he is merely following an impulse that had its origin in the beginnings of civilization. This urge to present a wish pictorially is, perhaps, as old as visual memory and the ability to wish. So primary is this desire that it has found its refinement in the written symbols of languages. The earlier a people's civilization, the more apt are we to find its written language in the form of ideagraphs. In this connection, it is interesting to observe that the Greeks seem to have considered *drawing* and *writing* as essentially the same process, using the same word, γράφειν for both.

Isn't it obvious that, at least in this sense, anyone can draw? Every traveler has resorted to picture writing, at one time or another, to describe some scene visited—and the use of the tablecloth as a canvas to illustrate a motor or a new golf club seems to be universal even in the most prosaic of individuals. These are the uses of drawing as a means of symbolic or literary expression. No one can deny the *ability* to draw in this sense; nor can anyone deny the *desire* to draw for this purpose. We have all done it. But this, you say, is not the kind of drawing we mean. We want to draw trees and river banks and the human form. Can anyone do that?

At this point, I suppose, a distinction should be made between drawing used to convey the wish of the child or the idea of the adult, and drawing as the direct and only means of expressing the beauty of form.

When drawing is employed to tell a story it succeeds only in so far as it conveys that story to the looker. It does not matter whether the figures are well composed or drawn. The pictures we see in the *New Yorker* and *Esquire* would not be more amusing if done by Michelangelo or Rembrandt, perhaps not as much. These drawings are merely story telling. (In this connection it is really amazing to note how poorly some of these stories are told pictorially. The perfect drawing of this kind would need no subtitle to explain it. Much remains to be done in this field.) The wit of the illustrator does not preclude an ability as a draughtsman, but it must be remembered that these values are distinct.

Let us say, quite simply, that the representation of form only is the purpose of drawing. In this sense, drawing has a content that cannot be expressed in words. The impulse to draw is akin to the exhilaration felt in the flight of birds or the arc of the golf ball in the air. It arises from a sense of form without reference to literary value, color or symbolism. Drawing is the art (and by that I mean craft) of rendering pictorially one's ideas of the forms of nature. It is not the purpose of this brief introduction to discuss the development of drawing from the primitive, two dimensional through the corporeous conception of form of the able draughtsman by which he interprets the solid objects of nature, back to the pseudo primitive, the forced naive, concept of the so-called modern.

12

First and foremost it is necessary to see the form as a whole, have it indelibly stamped in one's eye so that one feels its solidity, its three dimensional quality. Donatello expressed this perfectly when he said: "Pupils, I give you the whole art of sculpture when I tell you to draw.". . .

Perhaps we can now answer the question asked before: can we draw trees, river banks and the human form? If I must answer categorically, yes! If one has achieved that feeling for form, I can only call three dimensional, plus the desire to draw, the answer again is, yes.

The criterion, "I don't know much about art, but I know what I like", cannot obtain to draughtsmanship. Drawing can be criticized by demonstration and is based on knowledge. There is no easy short cut to good drawing. It entails work and practice based on sound principles and knowledge. But how gratifying the achievement, how satisfying the creation of form.

I know of no one more capable or worthier of imparting this knowledge than Arthur Zaidenberg. Years ago, when a very young man, he visited my *atelier* in Paris. Already he had a fine feeling for form and a sure hand. It was with the greatest interest that I saw him develop, achieving a place finally in the permanent collections of the finest museums in America. His work as an artist and teacher has developed surely and swiftly.

Now he comes to me with this book. "Anyone Can Draw" is more than an effort to impart the knowledge of draughtsmanship which he possesses to so great a degree. It is a conscious effort to enable all to see and express form with the freshness and vigor of the truly young.

New York, 1939

13

Foreword

BY GEORGE GOMBARTS
PRINCIPAL, SCHOOL OF INDUSTRIAL ART,
NEW YORK CITY

While there is no royal road to success in art, the path has been made somewhat less difficult for the traveler—both inexperienced and otherwise—by the publication of this latest approach to the study of figure drawing.

For many decades, students have spent much time and energy in drawing from the cast and in the minute study of anatomy. They were so awed by the prospect of drawing from the figure, that they approached this all-important phase of their art training with fear and trepidation. Now they may drop their timidity and take up the study of the figure with confidence and delight.

While planned primarily for the student, "Anyone Can Draw" is of inestimable value to those who are, or have been, academically trained in the figure but lack knowledge of drawing the lower animal life—dogs, horses, etc.

The need for a more thorough knowledge of figure drawing is evident in the work of many of our artists. The work of the illustrator in both men's and women's fashions places emphasis upon the figure. A knowledge of the figure is likewise essential in the fields of industrial art, book illustration, mural decoration, poster design, etc.

For many years, while principal of the New York Evening School of Industrial Art, I have observed that classes in figure

14

drawing—drawing from the draped and nude model—have been most largely and regularly attended.

In the days of the Godey's *Magazine and Lady's Book,* the drawings were naive and could never meet the critical standards of today's directors or agencies using sketches either for magazine, catalog or newspaper work. The figures underlying the costumes are impossible and unhuman. They clearly show that the artists had little or no knowledge of the figure.

After many years, during which artists work solely from memory, they are compelled to return to a fresh study of the figure so as to keep up the quality of their work. It cannot be denied that figure drawing becomes stylized if the artist does not return from time to time to actual drawing from the model. (The next best thing for him is to turn to one of the many excellent plates with which "Anyone Can Draw" is replete, for such inspiration as he may momentarily require.)

It should not be forgotten that the book is planned as an aid to the weak sister, to the tyro, as well as to the more advanced worker in the field of art. It does not take the place of first hand observation. It does not supplant the figure, but supplements it. It is a crutch to the helpless and should be resorted to in time of need and stress.

The many plates with which the book is filled are done in a very striking technique which is certain to appeal to the draughtsman. But while the plates are executed in such glamorous treatment, let the student beware of mere imitation. Each reader should develop his own technique. Only in this way will the book prove its worth. *Do not imitate; be yourself!*

Heretofore only specialists have attempted to do animals.

Mr. Zaidenberg attempts to show—and does so quite successfully—that a drawing of the human figure can be carried over easily to drawing the lower animals—dogs, horses and deer. The plates show very succinctly how they are related in action and construction. "Anyone Can Draw" should become a handy and ready reference book for both artists and students.

The text has been reduced to a minimum, as the plates are almost self-explanatory. The author, a young man, adds "Anyone Can Draw" to the large number of books already on the market, and contributes something definitely worthwhile. I believe he has succeeded in his attempt to make figure drawing somewhat less difficult and much more attractive.

In these days when increased opportunities are offered by state and municipality to those who wish to undertake work in the arts, the book comes as a windfall. It is decidedly refreshing and with its newer approach should further stimulate such study. Due to the current art renaissance—its appreciation, study and application—schools, colleges and universities have instituted new, up-to-date courses both for laymen, students and advanced workers. The State has become a patron of the arts. Sculptors, painters and architects are engaged upon thousands of projects in which figure drawing plays a most important part. Never before in the history of this country has such a widespread art interest been known.

To the thousands who will use "Anyone Can Draw," I wish much joy and pleasure. I feel certain that they will profit greatly from it. They will obtain much definite information concerning the human form and they will become better acquainted with the horse and the dog and other animals.

16

ANYONE CAN DRAW!

Anyone Can Draw!

Anyone can draw! That statement is almost as startling as it is true. Yet even the briefest glance at the pages that follow will demonstrate how, by this simple new method, there is no one who cannot become an adequate artist.

The ability to draw is not necessarily predetermined by any inherited artistic sense, by some strange quirk of fate, or even, as so many people are wont to believe, by that very rare phenomenon known as "talent." It may be true, however, that when the individual is possessed of one or more of the above-mentioned qualities he may perhaps go further in his chosen field, perhaps achieve that remote and mysterious sanctum reserved for "genius."

But it is not with such inspired natures that we are concerned. And we have no traffic with those authorities who prescribe, as prerequisites in artistic training, a vermin-infested attic, an inadequate supply of food, and an unappeased hunger for Beethoven symphonies. These things create atmosphere in the novels of Bohemia, but beyond that they are of little use. Certainly they have no place on the drawing board.

Our own essentials are much simpler. They consist of two eyes that can see, and a hand strong enough to hold a pencil. These are the implements. With them, and with this book, anyone should be able to draw. We most emphatically do not

19

mean to imply that every reader will be transformed into a Rembrandt, a Velasquez or a Renoir. The elemental make-up of such creative geniuses is too varied, too subtle, to be inducted by any series of words and sketches. No book can impart the unerring line of Rembrandt, the distinctiveness of Albrecht Dürer, or Velasquez' perfect feeling for values. To reach such noble heights is the destiny of very few out of the millions who may aspire.

However that may be, it should in no way detract from one simple truth: by following the instructions contained in this book, anyone will be enabled to tell a story with his pencil or brush, anyone will be enabled to draw human figures, animals and objects in sufficient detail to render them recognizable for what they are meant to be. This book deals with the basic approach to any and all drawing, the firm foundation upon which all great structures must needs be built. At the conclusion of this course, the student will be able to draw his figures proportionate and true in action.

Much depends on the individual himself. Imagination, perception, execution—all these play their parts; but, for the student, most important is application. Just as we cannot gauge the components inherent in a great artist, so we may not set limits which industry will not surpass.

The student should not be content to satisfy himself with copying the exercises outlined in this book. Constant observance of the figure and additional artistic endeavor will increase his ability to a very great extent. From the following chapters the student will learn to present the forms of the body and limbs in such a manner as to allow for superimposing any

20

amount of detail that he desires or is able to add in time.

This superimposed detail may be as unlimited as the imagination of the artist, and these pages will contain no rules of limitation. The artist must make that decision himself. His own good taste, his own knowledge, his own artistic sensibilities will dictate that decision. But the added detail need not break down the conventional forms which are demonstrated here, nor will the forms hamper the further advancement of the drawing.

There is no necessity for memorizing each of the simple forms demonstrated. Instead of searching out each muscle, bone, protuberance and wrinkle, try to acquire the feeling for simplification and the manner of analyzing the body forms, learning to see them in large planes. Practice the drawings illustrated, of course, but make every effort to draw from life whenever the opportunity offers, applying the principles outlined.

One not inconsiderable difficulty arises from the method of presenting each detailed portion of the figure by itself: the unit appears to stand alone, bearing no relation to the rest of the figure. This is understandably harmful, for the artist who learns in this manner sometimes encounters trouble when he attempts to assemble the whole.

And yet, despite this danger, no book previously published has ever even tried to correct the abuse. We know that it is impossible to introduce coordination in the illustrations, but it can be incorporated in the text. And so the earnest student will do well to read carefully each chapter before he takes his pencil in hand. In that way, not only will he grasp the thought behind each individual lesson, but he will understand more thoroughly the relationship of each unit to the complete figure.

Early in his studies the artist should learn to form a clear mental picture of his model. The first stages of his development in drawing are steps toward enriching this mental picture through serious research. The mental picture should include the figure in its entirety, so that no matter what minor form may attract the eye or what design the hand may trace upon the paper, the nature of the part to the whole may first be established.

An artist is primarily concerned with the external and the apparent. He views the things of nature as composed of color, tone, texture and light and shade, but behind this first concern, whether he be figure painter or illustrator, he requires certain things in order that he may render the human figure successfully. He must use his knowledge of structure skillfully; he must have an understanding of action and possess an insight into human character. All of this requires a definite amount of study, not all of which may be obtained from books.

One thought cannot be stressed too strongly. In drawing, as in every other field of endeavor, an open mind should be the base for every operation. Try not to have any preconceived ideas about what a figure looks like, how a leg is constructed, why we have ears. The truth of the matter lies in that each model is different: we must draw what we see when we see it.

In concluding this introduction, we shall use but one word to sum up the chief attribute towards artistic success, and that is "concentration."

22

PART ONE

The Figure

Leonardo da Vinci once wrote:

"A man, in his infancy, has the breadth of his shoulders equal to the length of his face, and to the length of the arm from the shoulder to the elbow, when the arm is bent. It is the same again from the lower belly to the knee, and from the knee to the foot. But, when a man is arrived at the period of his full growth, every one of these dimensions becomes double in length except the face, which, with the top of the head, undergoes but very little alteration in length. A well-proportioned and full-grown man, therefore, is ten times the length of his face; the breadth of his shoulders will be two faces, and in like manner all the above lengths will be double."

Without detracting one cubit from da Vinci's stature as an artist, we advise that his statement must be taken for what it is worth; it is only approximate, for, obviously, no hard and fast rules can apply to all figures, with their differences of proportion; in fact, the fewer rules the better, if one wants to draw fearlessly and with expression.

We believe that this simple method may better serve your purpose. It is, namely, a method of seeing imaginary lines and angles from point to point on the figure that may be before you at the time. This is really a matter of linear deductions and reasonings, founded upon the true judgment of the degree of

23

an angle formed by bisecting lines, and is an infallible system, provided one has trained oneself to imagine and "see" such angles correctly.

The direction of a straight line is less difficult to judge than that of a curve full of subtle contours. Academic accuracy does not necessarily imply a good drawing—in fact, to an artist it can be downright bad, for without inspiration or "style" such a drawing is too often flat. Raphael was sometimes incorrect in his proportions; Michelangelo oftener; Bouguereau never. Yet, which of the three do you consider the greatest artist? Our own academicians are not always impeccable, which should bring some consolation to the struggling art student.

In studying the figure as a whole, it is interesting to note how secondary the component parts become in their relation to the entire figure. They still retain their value, beauty, delicacy or strength, but in relation they assume a less imposing aspect. They actually take their subordinate place when viewed as parts of that vital quality which holds our attention when we see a figure in action.

That is because, in the infinite variety of action of which the human figure is capable, the lesser parts fuse into the greater in the most subtle manner, leaving us in doubt as to which of them is the more important for pictorial use. In that way the lines which surround the smaller parts melt into the larger and become a part of them. This is true of every degree of form, from the minutest detail to the largest mass; each form becomes a part of something larger than itself. Any form, no matter how important it may seem in itself, may be so submerged in a strong action as to lose the greater part, perhaps all of its importance.

24

But no amount of written explanation can demonstrate as forcibly and clearly as actual drawings, and the examples illustrated in this volume should prove much more beneficial to the student who is a little uncertain as to what to look for, and suggest to him how he may proceed.

Now the theory of figure construction as presented here is based on the premise that an exhaustive study of anatomy to familiarize oneself with the skeleton and the function and placement of each and every muscle is entirely unnecessary. Our driving motive is to be able to express the "intention" of a figure; not to render it in as finished and photographic a form as possible.

By "intention" we mean the action and general character of the figure. Every figure must express some sort of an idea; therefore, every figure will necessarily possess some "intention."

If you want to show men fighting or working or playing, it is essential that you draw figures which register those actions. Do not make portraits of individuals who just happen to be doing those things. In other words, it is the action that counts; not the likeness of the model. Of course, the figures you draw must have reasonable proportions, so that they will not be distorted beyond recognition of their original forms.

The following exercises are planned to help you to arrive at generalizations which will allow you to draw figures expressing your basic ideas in proportion and action. Each of the plates will contain a conventionalized form, reduced to its essence, as a guide upon which you may build your figure or detail.

Approach the beginning of your drawing of the figure bravely. There is nothing to fear. You will probably make many bad drawings at first; that is to be expected. Even when you are an experienced artist you will produce some unsatisfactory work now and again. No artist achieves perfection every time he sets pencil to paper—not even the greatest of the great.

However, if you search for the essentials, using all your powers of discrimination and good taste, there is no reason why your first drawing cannot be a good one.

This is what you must do:

Pose a model. Analyze the meaning of the pose. What is it intended to convey? Strong action? Repose? Determine its character and concentrate on getting the essence of it. Place the head—just an oval—on the strong parallels of the neck joined to the center of the shoulder line. Find the direction of the shoulder line. Swing in the oblong of the torso to the waist line.

Get the direction of the imaginary line of the hips. If the figure is standing, find the point of support for the weight of the figure—which foot? Or is it both? Find the base line. Place it and make sure that the strong shafts of the legs (even if they are indicated merely by parallel lines) are planted firmly on that base.

If this is done honestly and unpretentiously—without bringing into play any of your *a priori* knowledge of "art"—you will have achieved the primal desire of the artist: you will have expressed the salient features of an emotion, simply and directly.

Your first studies should resemble those on the next page.

26

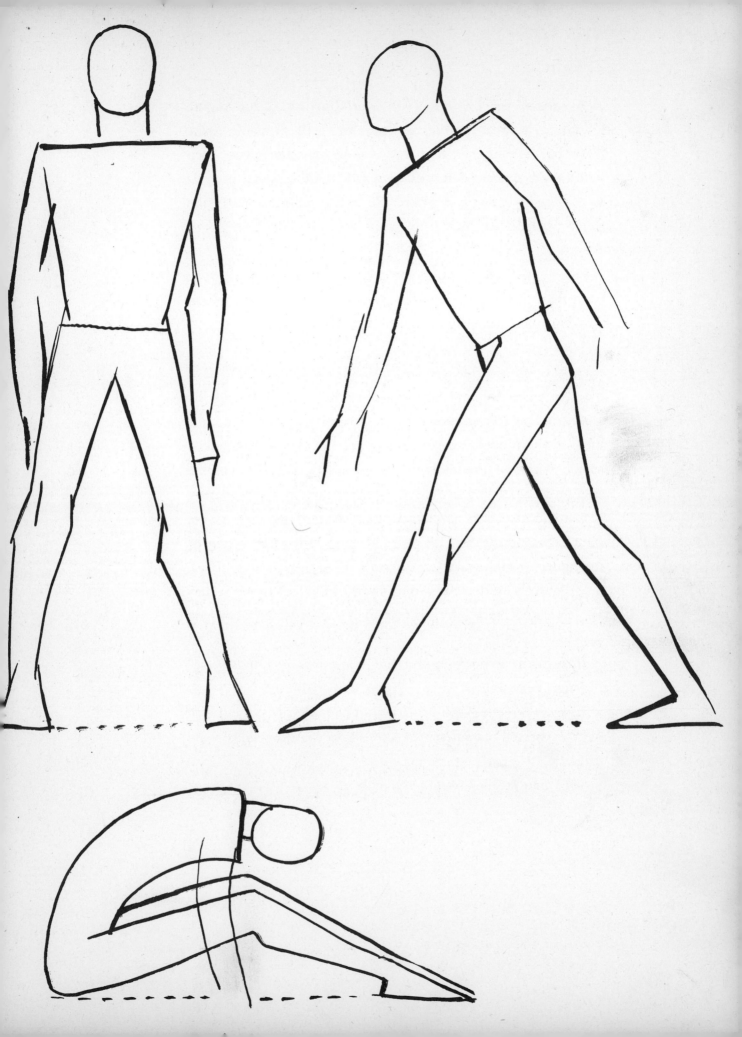

The Chest

In literature, the chest is a complicated structure. Centuries of authors have extolled the virtues and despaired of the villainies born therein.

But however interesting the subject may be for the physiologist or the philosopher, the artist may treat it with simplicity and confidence. For the large mass of this framework has no movement of its own and remains unchanged in any very material manner, no matter what action the figure assumes. And this is the form which will give solidity and bulk to your figure drawings.

But, for all its inflexibility, it must not be regarded too lightly. It is on the chest that so many important appendages and details will be added. A close scrutiny of the chest will reveal a myriad of ridges, depressions and muscles; planes into sections; and sections into even smaller areas. However, for our purpose, all these things must be ignored. Instead, treat the chest as one large, simple mass. In that way it will serve to balance the weight of the pelvis, which, in turn, carries the entire body.

When the model is standing erect, with his chest out, the plane of the shoulder is set well back of the chest. We can see that the chest, from the middle region of the shoulder girdle to the nipples at the base of the chest, makes a great plane broken

28

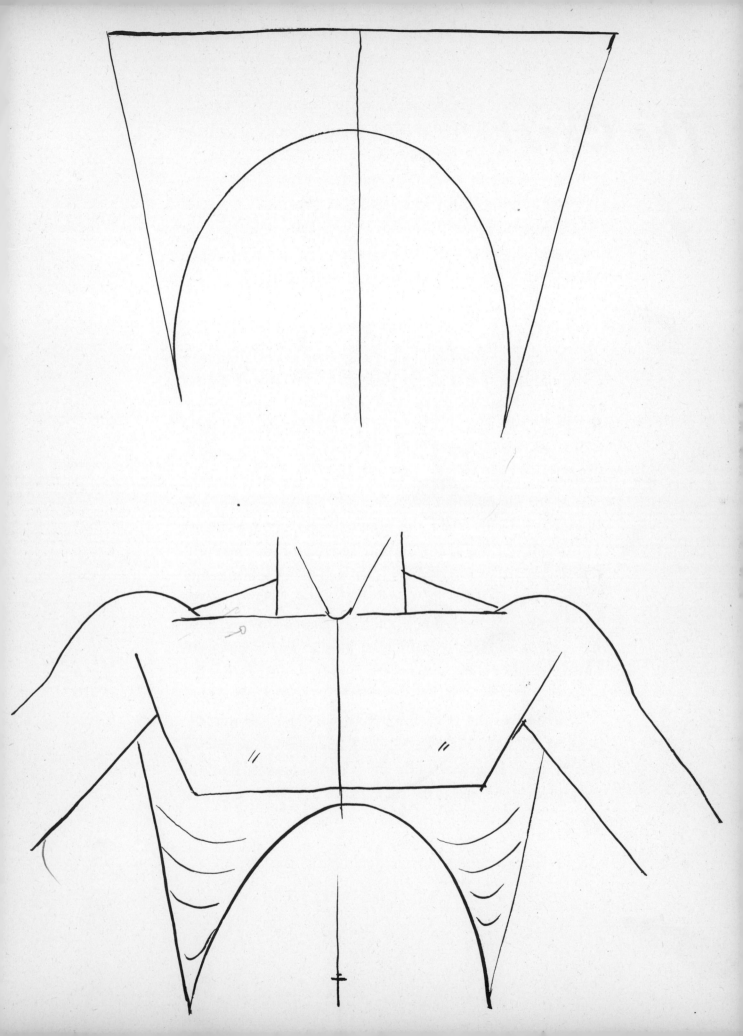

by the retiring shoulder, placed steplike but parallel, back of the plane of the chest; that is, the center of the shoulder is set back of the center of the body.

The student will do well to regard the chest as a sort of a permanent frame. The Greeks used it to admirable advantage. They had an uncanny feeling for rightness of spacing, with an exquisite control of line. This is observable in the figures on their vases of the Fifth Century B.C., in the simplicity of their line, perfect rhythm, and knowledge of movement.

Of course the ancient Greeks had more opportunities than we have of studying the human figure in its highest perfection, as, owing to lack of physical exercise, the majority of people nowadays carry superfluous fat. But since we shall be drawing people and not ideals, it is just as well that our models appear before us with the usual mortal's faults. It may be added, though, that the Greeks were not quite so perfect as their statues would have us believe. The common practice in those days was for the sculptor to use for his models a group of athletes. From one he would copy the torso; from another the legs; a third provided the head; and so it went until the completed statue represented the best features of perhaps a score of athletes. Details were important in those days because the artist was seeking to represent the inhabitants of Olympus, not the men of the earth.

In drawing the chest, remember that the spine is the pliant, moveable hinge on which the torso swings. The breast is superimposed upon the rib cage; it is not a part of the fundamental structure.

30

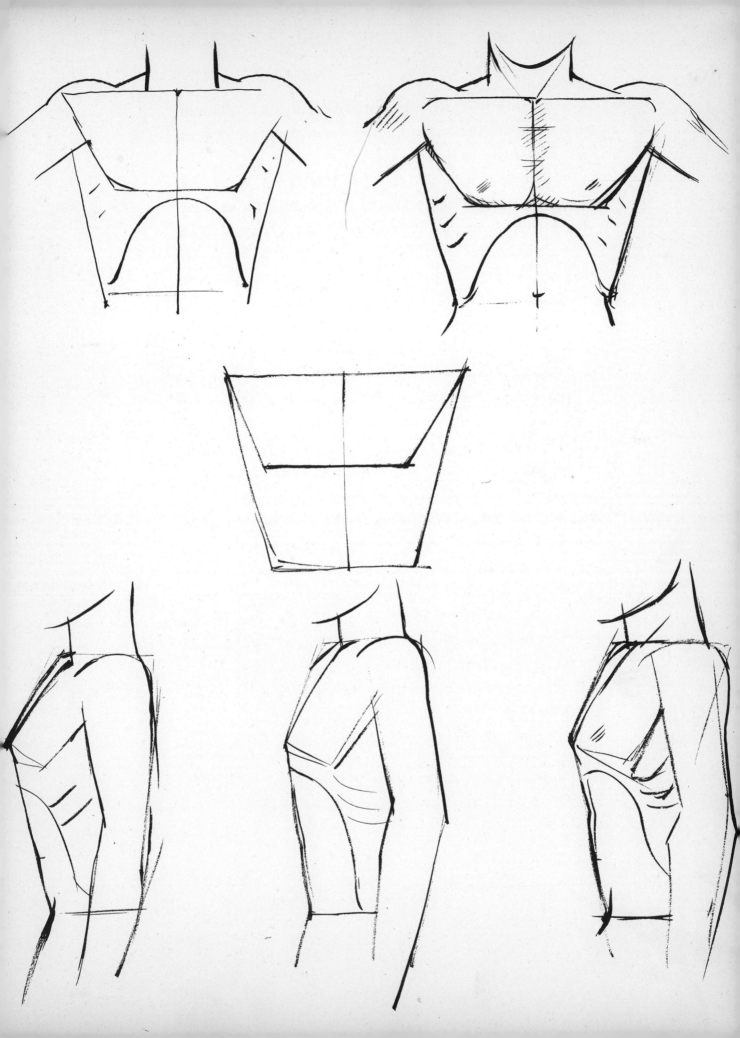

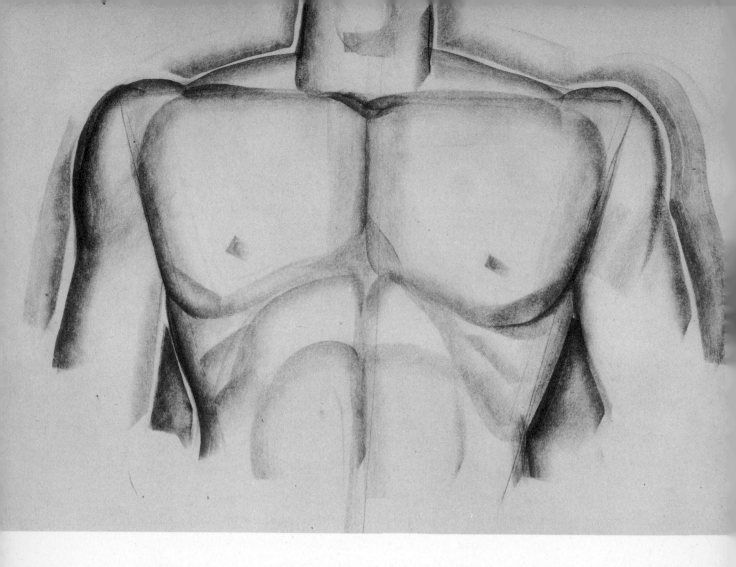

We arrive at this shaded study of the torso by following the stages outlined in the previous plates: the rib cage, the fixed line of the shoulders and the oblong form of the breast superimposed.

It serves to demonstrate how a few minutes' work on the simple understructure can change it into a "finished" drawing by bringing to the shading the same analytical process as we used in the understructure; that is, we worked out the pattern of the form or shadow, avoiding all extraneous detail.

The Shoulder

Reduced to its basic form, the shoulder should be drawn as a straight line across the collarbones from one side of the chest to the other. Then add two sloping sides, placing the apex in the center of the column of the neck.

That may sound quite simple. And, in reality, it *is* quite simple. Yet it is just as simple to commit errors which will subsequently throw your entire drawing out of line. This happens with practiced professionals as well as with beginners.

One famous example of this common error was handed down from the Fifteenth Century by the painter Marricini in his murals for the Scarfa Cathedral near Milan. In the main group on the south wall of the Chapel kneels the commanding figure of Saint John. His torso is turned so that he appears in a position a little more than three-quarters full. One arm is raised in benediction; the other hangs limply at his side. But Marricini was probably so intent about the position of these arms that he neglected the shoulders from whence they sprung. As a result of this misplaced eagerness, the shoulders form anything but a straight line. And so to even the most casual observer Saint John appears a hopeless and repulsive cripple.

Other great offenders were Del Sarto and, in one instance, even the master-draughtsman Ingres. But the list is too long to set down here; we mention these errors only to stress the fact that no one is immune from making them, and that only by great vigilance can they be avoided.

The student who is too aware of light and shadow will be the most apt to falter. Light and shadow are, of course, very important, but they really do not influence bone structure in any way whatsoever. Another common mistake is made when the student tries to draw the shoulder in two different planes. Incredible as it may sound, this happens quite often.

The recurrence of this last error is the more understandable when we remember that the neck sometimes appears as a point of division. It is then that the beginner, and apparently the professional too, throws the two halves of the shoulder on divergent angles, on different planes.

Therefore it becomes increasingly necessary first to indicate the position of the shoulder with one broad sweep of the pencil, one stroke of the brush. The artist must learn also to ignore the parallel columns of the neck. In no instance may the neck serve as a point of division. To avoid confusion, pencil the line of the shoulders before sketching in the lines of the neck.

Remember that the whole form is a triangle. The direction of the base line of the shoulders must be determined early in the placing of your figure; otherwise the various connecting lines and jutting angles may serve to confuse you.

Methods of approach are shown in the following plate.

34

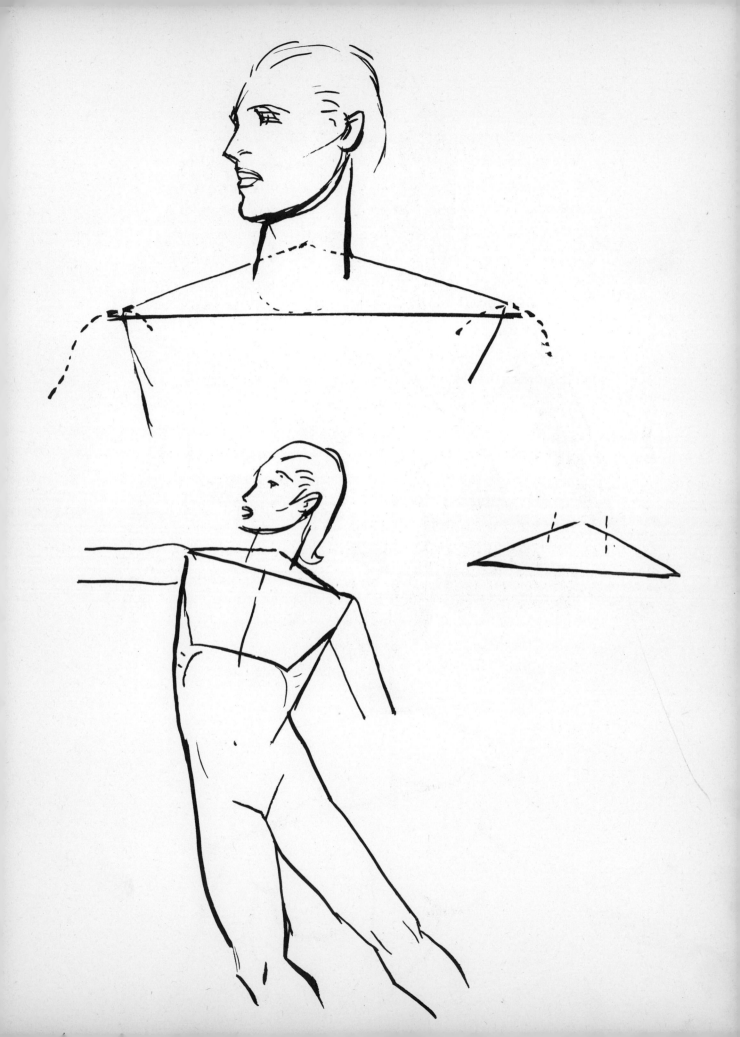

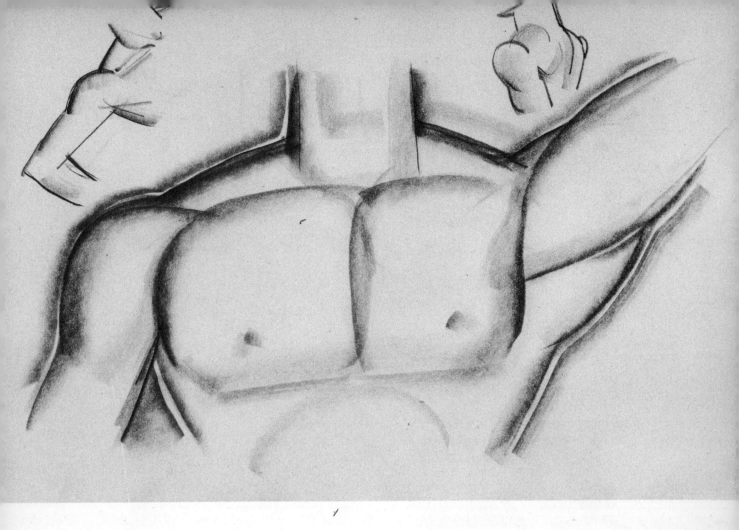

In studying the shaded shoulder, notice that because the line of the bones across the top of the chest form is close to the surface, we are aided in getting well defined shadows. The strongly shadowed portion is necessarily obscured by some protruding form.

You must seek out these depressions and protuberances, making the most of the larger, more important ones. Elimination in this process is just as important as it is in the study of line forms.

37

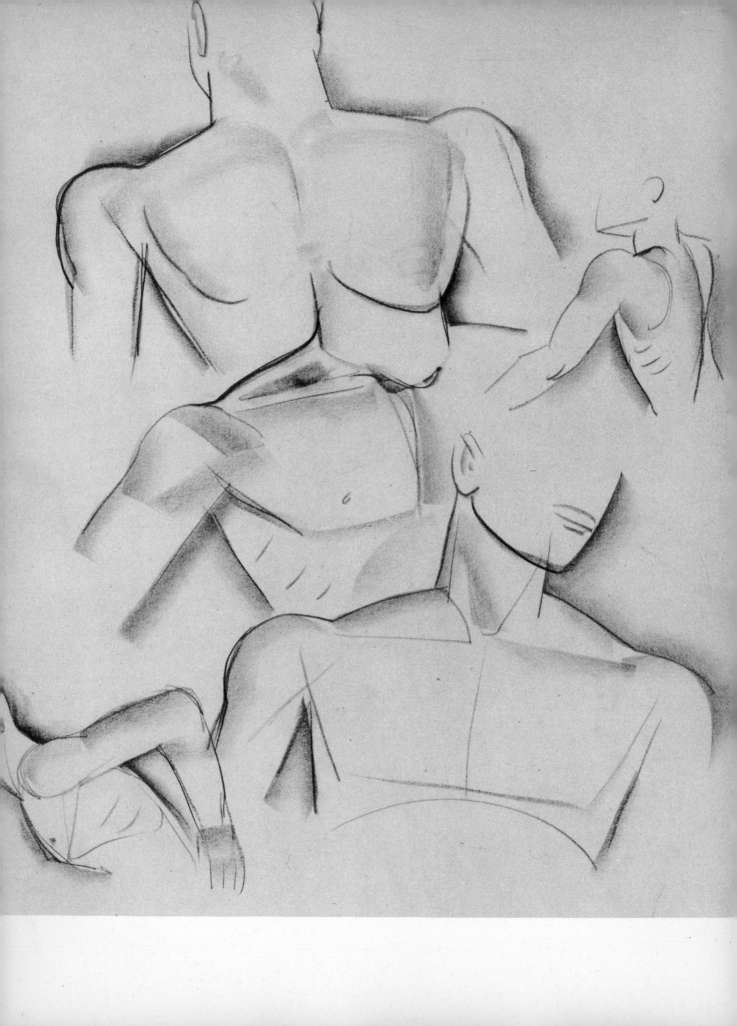

The Back

The back is the straight line of the shoulder to the line of the hips. The sides taper to the hips, and so an oblong is formed. Bisecting this oblong is the line of the spine. That is the back.

Its form cannot vary much, no matter what the action of the figure. And yet we have all met people whose backs are at least as expressive as their features. When we recall that backs are usually seen clothed, while features are generally uncovered, this portion of the anatomy takes on a new importance. Nor is a scientific explanation necessary.

The great sculptors of classic antiquity knew little about anatomy from either the scientific point of view or in the deep sense of post-mortem examination. Their marvellous anatomical exactness was obtained by the frequent opportunities they had of seeing the nude human body in action, displayed in the gymnasium. The study of external forms alone, in their constant change, gave the Greek sculptors their extraordinarily correct knowledge.

Today, when we have to work in the streets or other public places, it is rather impractical to make actual measurements of the figure or figures we wish to draw. And we should risk being "run in" by the police if we attempted to tapemeasure utter strangers! So we must depend solely upon our eye as the only true means of arriving at good proportions. We must fix the principal characteristics and seize upon the most notable points and comparisons.

The unconscious model being clothed, and his body being therefore camouflaged, the student is apt to forget the structure hidden underneath, which is made apparent by the form that creases take and the shape of the figure shown where the clothes fit more tightly upon the flesh. He must calculate the change of appearance and proportion by foreshortenings, for the dimensions of the figure should principally be considered in lengths and divisions, in halves, and in even smaller measurements. Seldom, if ever, should any mechanical help or plumb line be employed, for such means interrupt the sight and are apt to cause us to lose our feeling for the figure as a whole.

For every student who wants his pictures to tell a story, and more especially for those who are interested in using their art for illustrative purposes, no little emphasis may be placed on the back for character delineation.

Now we are aware that a straight back is no more indicative of a noble soul than are widely-spaced eyes or the other patent stand-bys of the physiognomists. But art, as such, sometimes surmounts the realistic to the symbolical, and it is of that quality we speak.

For movement and action, remember that the back swings on the axis of the hips and on the flexible spine.

40

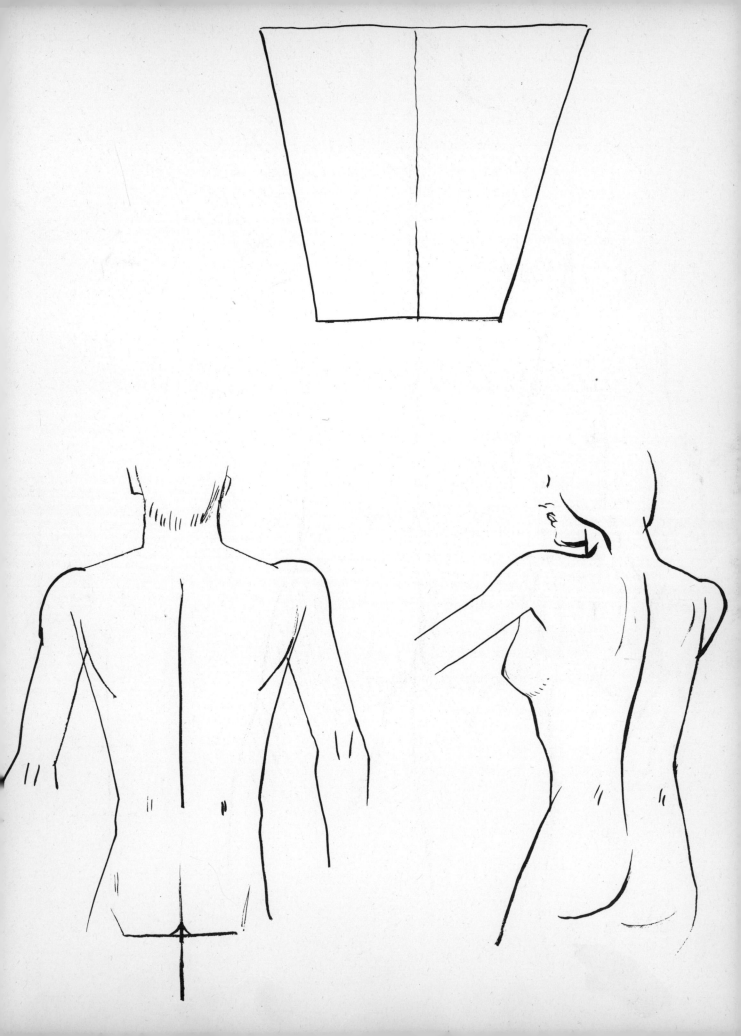

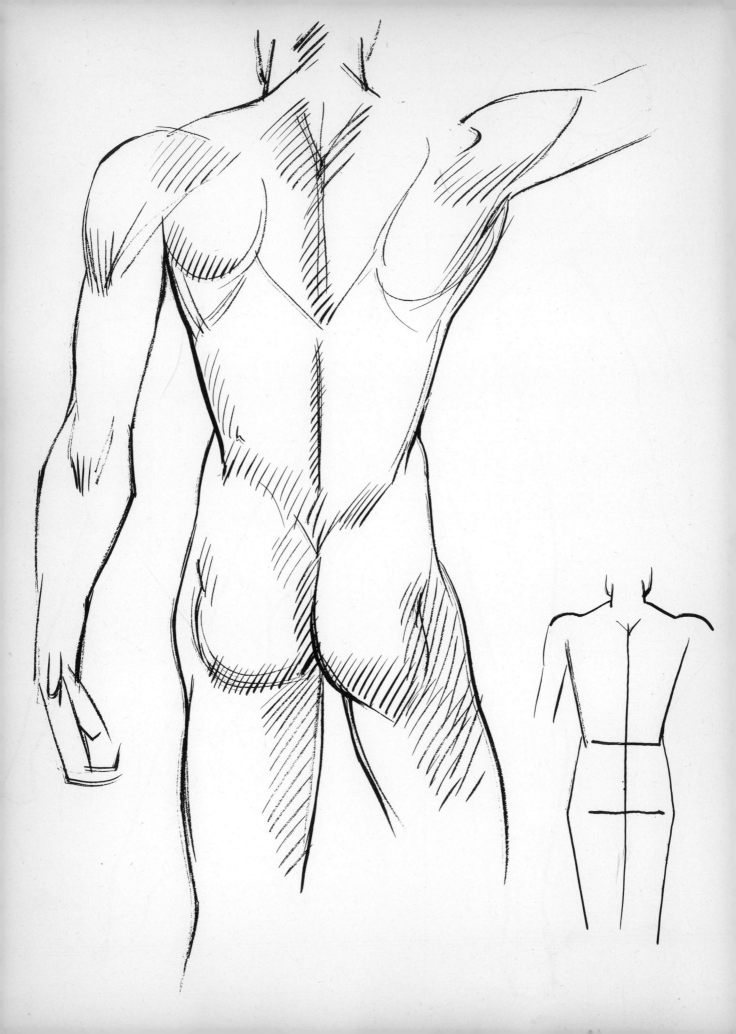

The Leg

The oblong form of the thigh diminishes in thickness as it approaches the knee. From the knee the leg widens to the middle of the calf, then tapers to the base of the calf. From the base of the calf to the ankle bone the lines descend in parallels. At the ankle bone the parallels descend into the top apex of the triangle formed by the foot. (See plate for these three forms.)

Compared with the arm, the degree of taper in the leg is greater, as the leg at the thigh is heavier compared with the ankle, than the upper arm compared with the wrist. In a general way, the changes that mark the diminishing widths are not dissimilar. The arm tapers slightly to the elbow; the leg, in proportion as it is heavier, tapers more rapidly to the knee; the mass of the calf more rapidly in proportion as the calves are heavier than the muscles of the forearm. In the leg, too, the alternation of flesh and bone are more noticeable than in the arm.

So much for the shape of the leg. However, in sketching it is not always necessary, in some cases not even advisable, to adhere strictly to this formal plan of structure. There will be times when a single line, perhaps even just the indication of a line, will serve your purpose to better advantage than a leg drawn in painstaking detail. But, of course, you must make sure that your one line does suggest the leg in its entirety. Brevity may be the soul of art as well as of wit, but even the

44

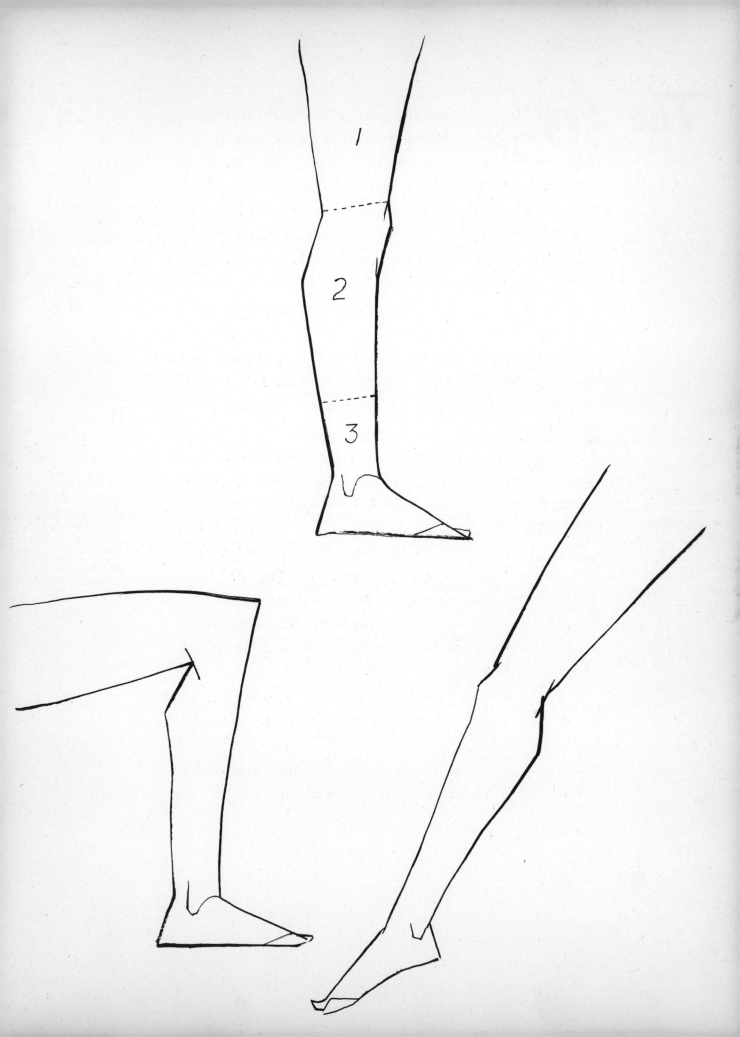

best story loses its point if it cannot be clearly understood.

In art, legs have a singular force. They are the tubes through which man draws his power, his sustenance from the earth. The great artists of all ages have recognized this fact, as we may glean from almost any one of their works.

But this power is not only mystical. There are excellent physical reasons for portraying strength in the lower limbs. If the pelvis supports the torso, then the legs support the entire body. And it does not require an especially brilliant architect to know that a house will be no stronger than its foundations.

In studying your model from a front view, you will notice that the outer lines of the legs are quite dissimilar. One line will descend straight from the hip; the other will form a convex curve.

Further study will prove that the convex lines appear on the side of the leg which bears the most weight, as the hip on that side is thrust out in order to bring the weight over the center of gravity.

When the muscles of the opposite side are relaxed, the hip drops an inch or two and the whole side (not including the small inequalities) assumes the general appearance of a straight line from the armpit to the ankle. When the line of the hips tips one way, the line of the shoulders generally tips in the other direction.

It can be said, in normal action, that the high hip will be under the low shoulder, and the low hip will be under the high shoulder.

It is well to consider the slant of the hips and the shoulders immediately after the construction lines are drawn.

46

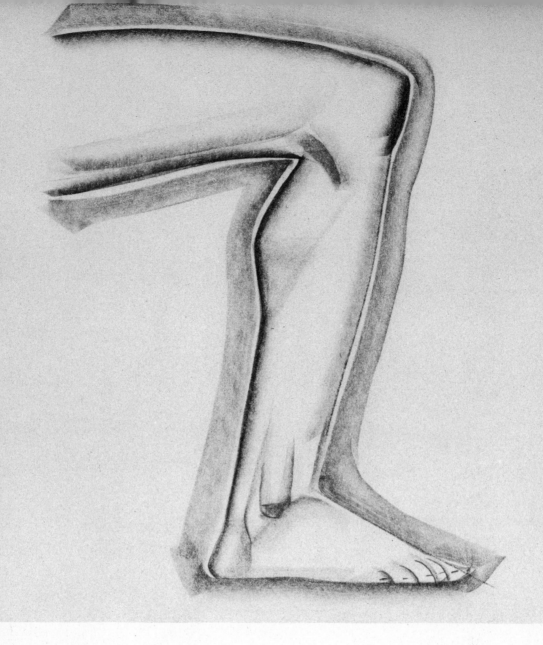

The more rugged surface of the male leg makes for a better study of the shaded forms; each muscle and tendon throws a shadow. Great strength and firmness can be shown by accentuating the calf muscle and its resulting shadow, the long lithe line of the tendon to the heel, and the strong muscle that runs the length of the thigh to the declivity at the back of the knee.

An occasional deep note, such as is under the protruding ankle bone or in the knee form, will make for a solid, toned study when combined with tones to denote curvature in the whole leg form.

The Foot

The foot is comparatively easy to draw when viewed from the side. It may be said to fit into a right angle, the back of the ankle being on the vertical line, the heel slightly outside the vertical line. The sole of the foot, extending along the base, may be said to fit into the convex and concave lines used for the figure, the instep being represented by the concave, and the flat of the foot by the convex line. Either of these plans will serve the purpose, but the use of both will give a very clear idea of the character of the whole shape of the foot.

A little difficulty arises when the foot is turned toward the observer and the perspective must be considered. The straight line at the base is used again, but it is no longer horizontal and its inclination must be very carefully considered, as it is this slant of the foot that most surely fixes the position of the figure in its relation to the observer. If the angle is wrong, even though the rest of the figure be perfectly drawn, the whole will appear to be weak and unbalanced.

From the front of the shin bone an out-curve is always found that ends in the ankle. On this curve the inside and outside lines of the calf of the leg may easily be constructed, and the lines of the foot will follow this curve with exactness.

In profile the foot is to be visualized as a triangle, as shown in the first figure following. In length it is about the same as

50

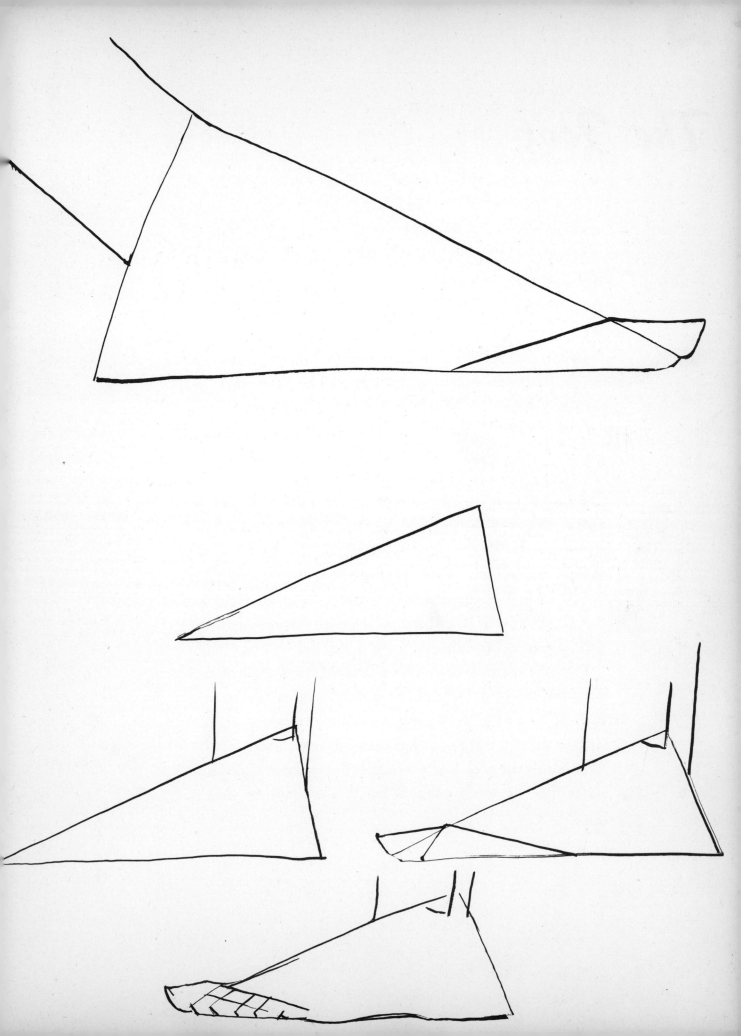

the length of the head from chin to top. The range of the toes and the junction with the ankle tend to change this form very little. The parallel lines of the ankle descending into the triangle will form a solid foundation for the weight of the figure.

The range of the small toes may also be visualized as a triangle. Within this form all the peculiar little twists of the toes take place. But do not let their apparent complications disturb you. Simply draw them in three forms very similar to the fingers, and for most purposes you will have indicated all you need. The great toe dominates the fore part of the foot. It is very much akin to the thumb and should be analyzed in the same manner.

The foot in front view is an oblong like the back of the hand in shape, although, of course, a good deal larger. Notice again how the form for the toes arbitrarily sets a limit for them, beyond which limit they do not extend.

Rotation of the foot at the ankle is not nearly so free as that of the hand at the wrist. It can be pointed forward in a straight line with the leg and also bent upwards to a right angle, but under no circumstances can it ever be depressed to the back of the leg.

Care should be taken so that the proportions of the foot will jibe with those of the figure. Not only the length but the breadth, too, must be considered. If there is no balance your drawing will take on the appearance of a caricature.

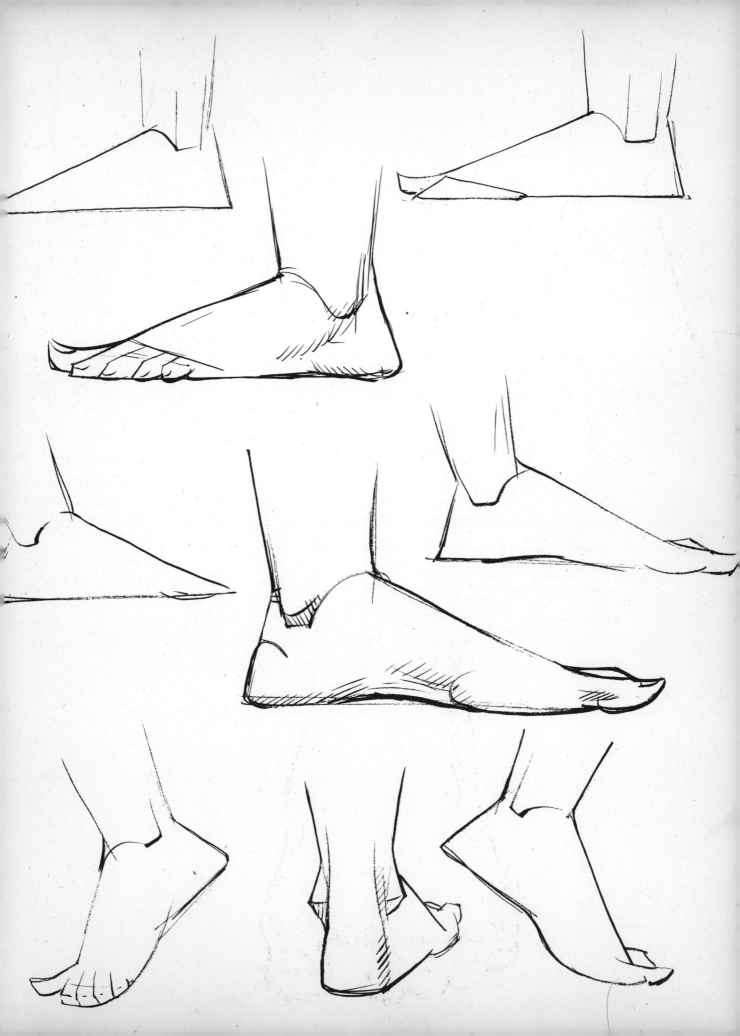

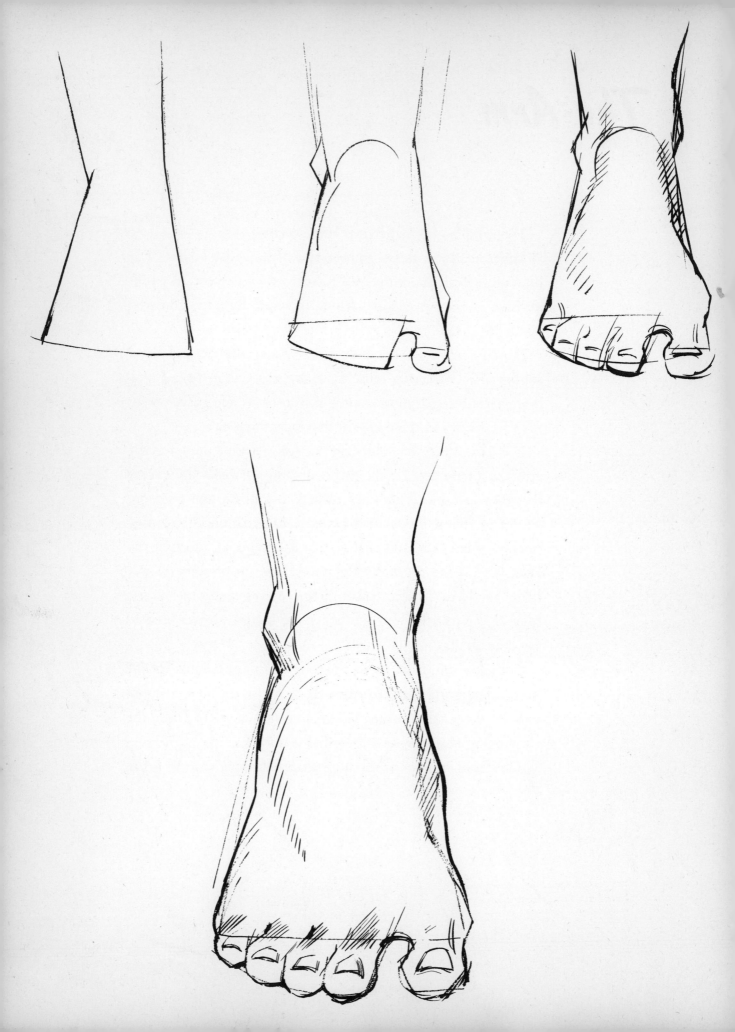

The Arm

The arm can be realized as three forms.

The forearm is heavy immediately below the elbow. The lines taper until about the mid-forearm, then descend in parallel lines to the wrist bone, which is where the arm joins the hand. (See plate.)

Muscles really do not bulge very materially beyond these confines. In indicating muscles, a slight curve on your frame line will suffice for most normal purposes. When great power is to be conveyed these curves may be exaggerated.

It is interesting to note that the construction lines for the arm are almost exactly the same as those of the body, except that they are shorter and are turned to a horizontal position.

Not too many models possess arms of great nobility or distinction. Many students realize that fact, and so, to offset the lack, use instead the statues of the Greeks or of some of our better moderns. In some cases these are exaggerations, but the play of the muscles and the bones are almost always used to good advantage.

The transition from muscle to long tendons accounts for the graceful tapering of the forearm. At the wrist, the bones coming close to the surface makes for greater angularity of form, the wrist being nearly twice as broad as it is thick.

The common error of the unpracticed draughtsman in forming the arm lies in drawing the parts too detached, giving the appearance of its being hung on at the shoulders, as on a doll, and as if broken at the elbow when the arm is bent. We have all seen drawings in which the wrist was not considered at all; too often the hand hangs from an arm minus a wrist.

When in action, the many parts of the arm show their intimate interrelation to one another. An artist's arm may almost be in repose, only the finger tips being used in executing some deft touch. But the next moment the action includes the whole length of the fingers, the wrist, elbow, including the act of pronation or supination, and finally the shoulder. He may make a master stroke requiring a sweep from the shoulder, but each joint, each set of muscles to the sensitive finger tips, lends its aid to give to the supple movement of his stroke the desired character and quality. So in a drawing, every part of the hand and arm must be in character both in form and action. No matter how definitely the forms may be distinguished, by name, location, shape and proportions, they must in practice interrelate under the surface of the continuous skin, sometimes lost through a connecting curve, sometimes accented by abrupt angularity, but always connected.

The arm must never seem pinioned, suggesting that it can only move parallel to the side of the body. The elbow in the flexed arm should not suggest through its irregularity that the arm has been broken in order to locate it. The point of the elbow should be found under the center of the shaft of the upper arm when the forearm is flexed upon the upper, and not on a line with the back of the arm. This continues the sense of connection.

56

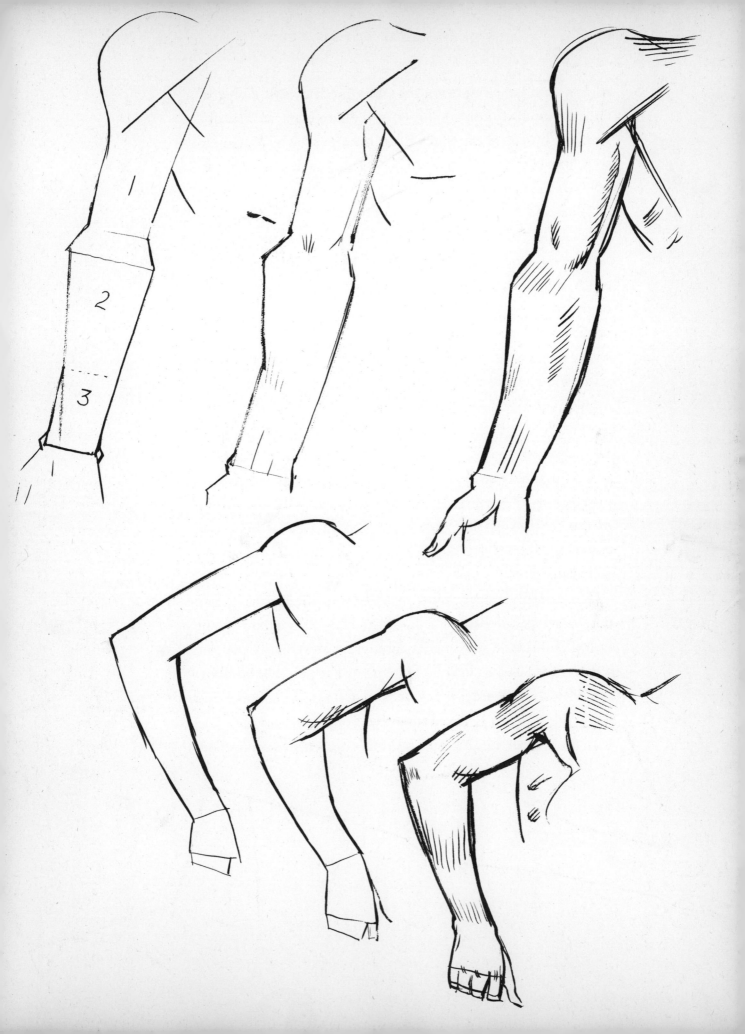

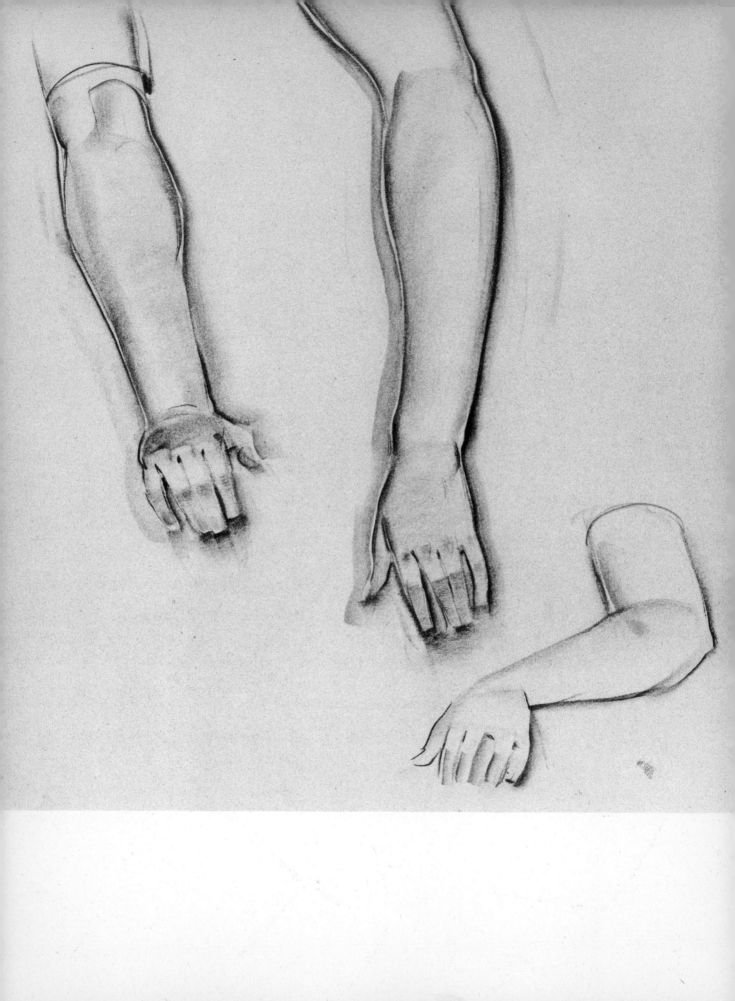

The Hand

Hands, even to the accomplished draughtsman, present more difficulties than faces. The character of a man or woman shows itself to some degree in the shape and state of his or her hands. These should be considered in conjunction, for they are co-related and express the same emotions.

The body of the hand is larger on the side of the thumb than on the side of the little finger, the palm is longer than the back, broader at fingers than near the wrist, and thicker at the wrist than near the fingers.

The back of the hand is quite flat except when the fist is clenched, though it assumes considerable convexity upon connection with the wrist. The palm, on the contrary, is like a shallow bowl with squared sides, well cushioned on both sides near the wrist.

Collectively the fingers taper, and the tip of the middle finger, the longest, forms the apex of the mass. Each finger tapers in itself with a tendency toward the middle finger, though when the hand is in action the middle and the third fingers are inclined to go together. The length of the first joint of the fingers is equal to the two remaining ones, but the palm extends halfway up the length of the first joint, giving the appearance on the inside of the fingers of all the joints being of equal length.

In the hand and foot, the bones of the fingers and toes are

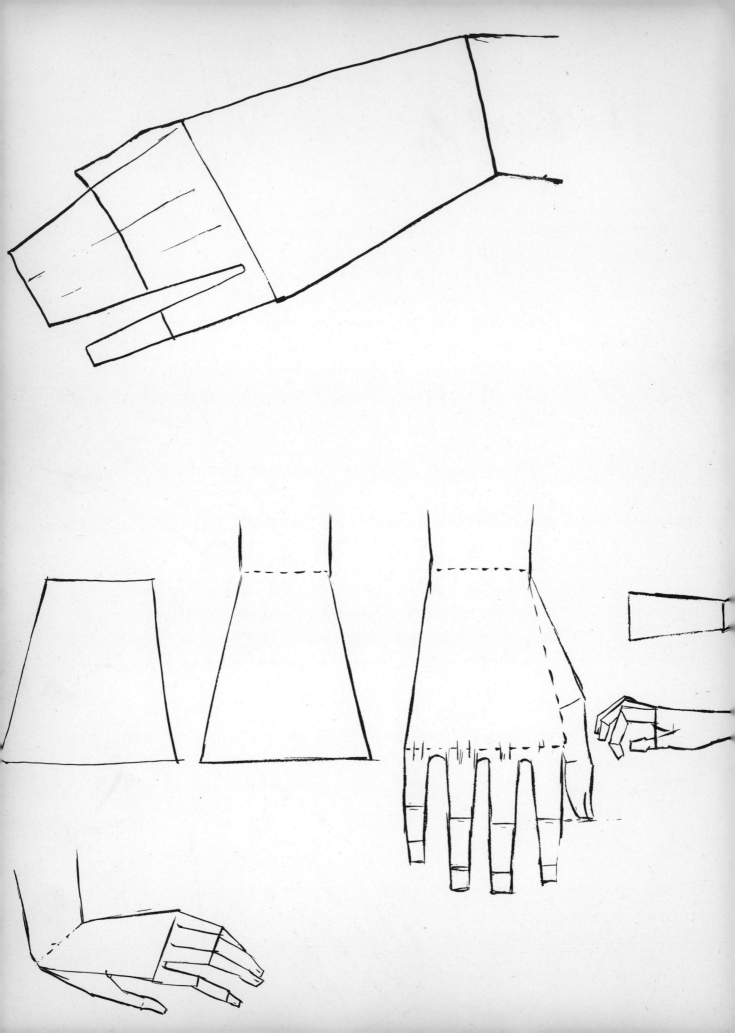

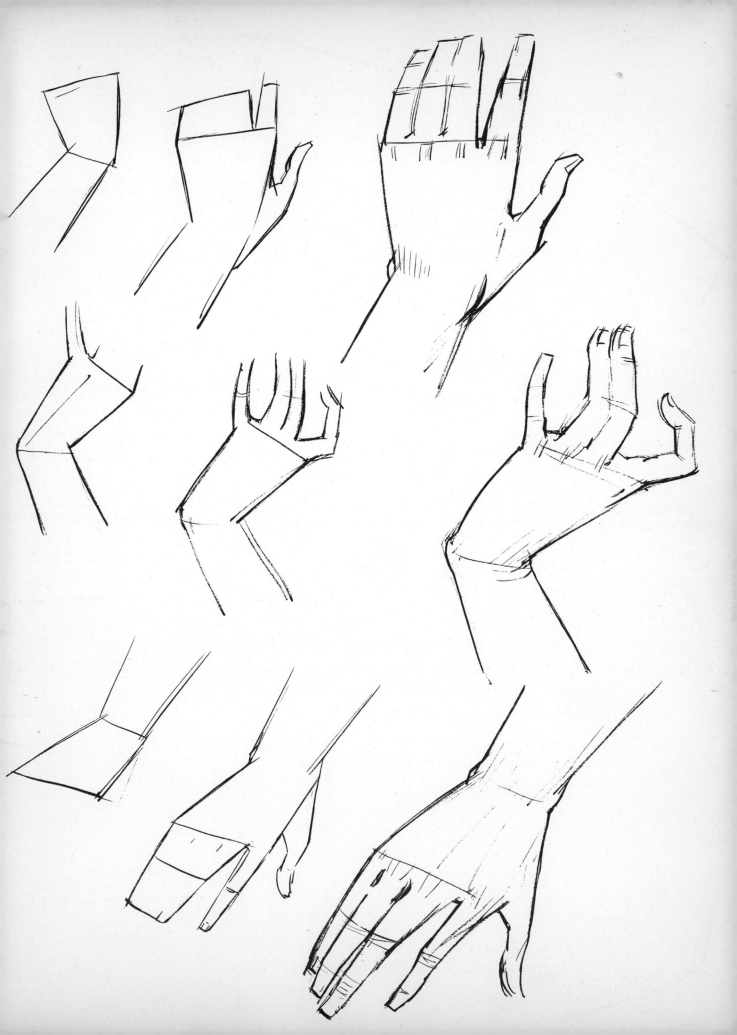

attached to a common center in somewhat the same manner as the ribs of a fan are held at the joint. As these bones are loose at one end, the number of positions that the fingers may assume is very great. It is very confusing to try to draw the hands and feet unless they are considered as part of some orderly scheme.

The correct drawing of the extremities needs close consideration and study. Many drawings in different positions should be made from life casts, as well as from the model. In portraits we frequently see these members slurred over or drawn without character. In Vandyke's portraits the hands are beautifully represented, although mostly of the same type, as his sitters were usually members of the nobility and aristocracy, who did little manual work and took pride in the beauty of their hands.

We particularly observe in old people the shape of the bones at the finger joints and wrists. The student should draw his own hands, in as many positions as possible, especially when foreshortened, as no better practice may be had. Before attempting to finish finger by finger, he should get the proportions by blocking in shapes and connecting the main forms by straight lines and angles. The sooner he can dispense with this method, however, the better.

The twisted look the muscles take in the forearm should not be overlooked, and the tendons working the wrist and hand should be carefully studied. Rotation at the wrist is full, much freer than with the foot at the ankle.

But sometimes, as in the case of Margaret McEnery, even the professional can carry the study of detail too far.

Miss McEnery, who has done notable work with both pencil

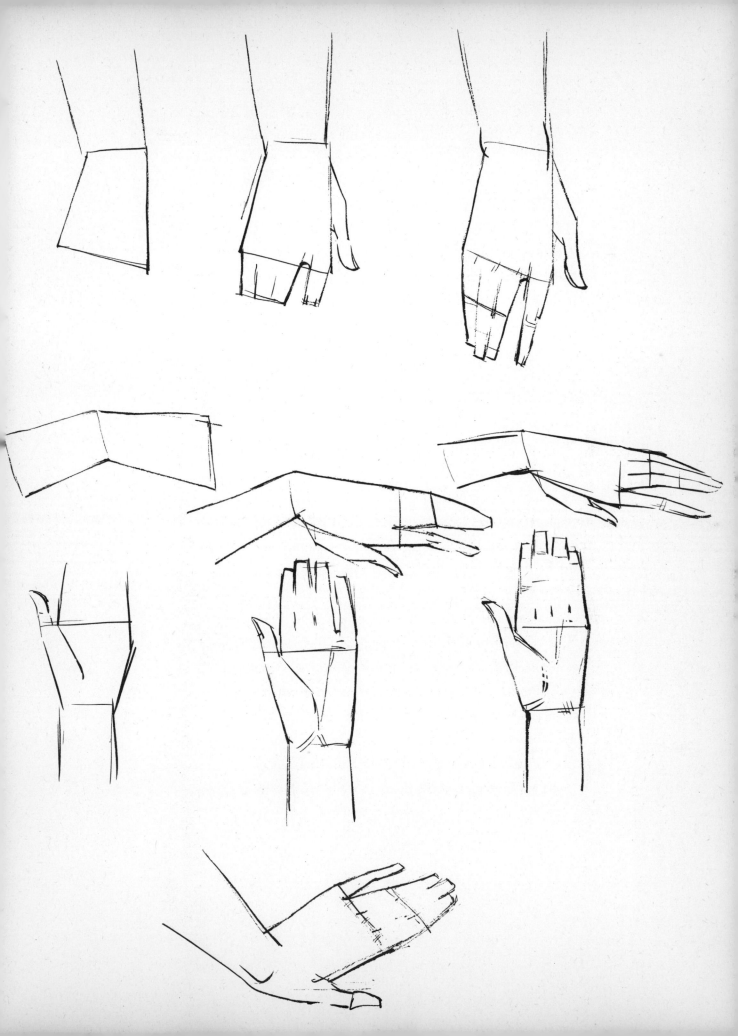

and water colors, had made rather a specialty of hands. At first her studies were remarkable for their charming simplicity. Then, gradually, more and more detail appeared. Soon her pictured hands were masses of fine lines, intricate networks. Then, abruptly, they ceased altogether.

Two years later Miss McEnery gave an exhibition at a New York gallery. The show consisted entirely of seascapes. Miss McEnery told reporters that she did not intend doing any more hands. "When I found myself studying palmistry," she said, "I decided I'd had enough."

For the beginner, these details should suffice:

Indicate the palm or the back of the hand as an oblong, the sides tapering slightly toward the parallels of the wrist as shown in the following plate. This oblong joins the wrist at the wrist bone. The wrist bone acts as a hinge for the whole hand.

Visualize the fingers as three separate parts which are joined at the knuckle bones. The fingers taper much less than they seem to; it is the nail which creates that illusion. Parallel lines suffice to indicate each finger. Do not make too much of the knuckles or the many wrinkles and lines in the skin. In expressing the hand, its mechanics are more interesting than these superficial details. Rather show the intention and purpose of the joints than the surface peculiarities. The thumb reaches to the middle joint of the first, or index, finger.

At first glance the hand seems the most difficult part of the human anatomy to draw, but it is so alluring as a decorative motive, and is so fascinating to draw, that it offers more than the usual inducements to the artist who works from it.

66

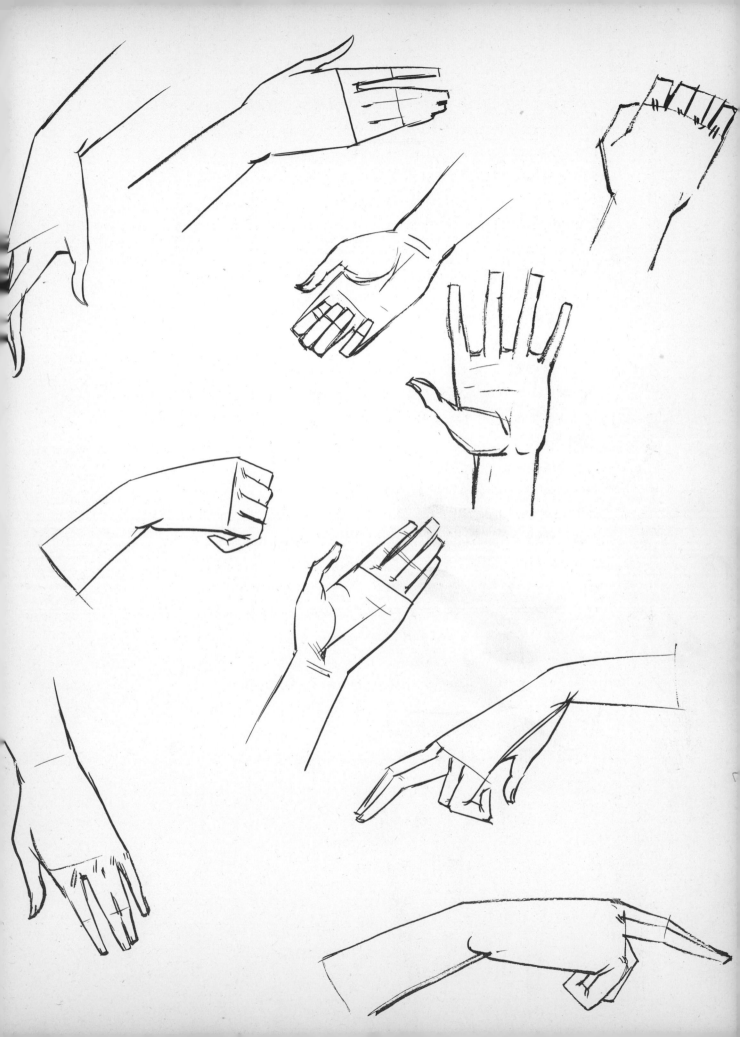

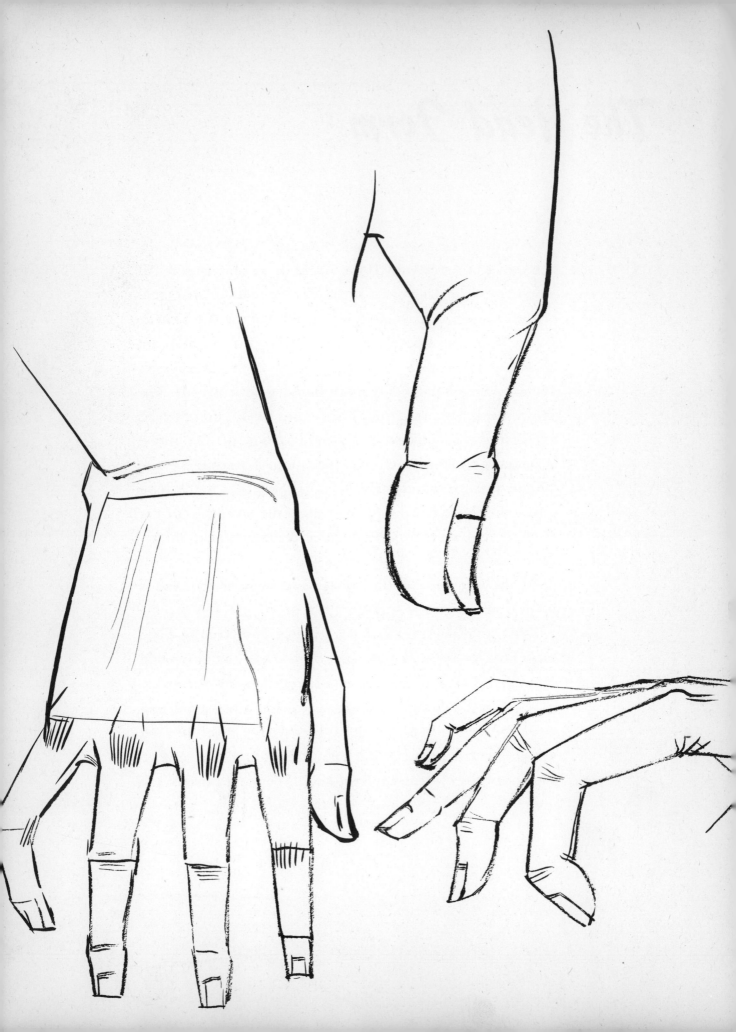

The Head Form

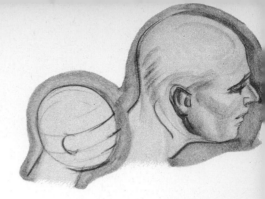

In drawing the head in profile disregard, for the time being, the eyes and the mouth. Think of the head only as a round decorative form, with one side flat, but with the sort of roundness that seems to be based on a square rather than on a circle.

The head is represented as being circular in form when not seen in profile. There are positions in which it seems almost round, although it is really much longer than it is wide. The bony structure from the front, on the same level as the observer, is elliptical or egg-shaped. As the head turns from this position it becomes wider through the center until it reaches the true profile, where it fits more nearly into a square. Up to the point where the cheekbone disappears behind the nose, the circular form seems to serve best. Beyond that point the square character is very apparent.

We may say, however, that the general shape of the head is an oval with a greater width at the top.

Draw faint lines to locate the features. Horizontally, three main lines locate the eyes, the base of the nose, and the mouth. Vertically, through the center of the oval, a line will pass between the eyes, down the nose, and will bisect the mouth and chin. The eyes are located half-way between the top of the head and the chin. The base of the nose is about half-way between the line of the eyebrows and the chin. The space between the eyes is equal to the width of one eye. Practice drawing these ovals with the features indicated lightly.

The lines that are drawn to locate the features may be regarded as circles which extend around the sphere of the head. When the head bends backward, the circles follow in perspective. They become ellipses and give foreshortening.

We can divide the head into two parts, inseparable one from the other, namely, the cranium or skull, and the face, each of which is ovoid in form. The face proper is what we see from the eyebrows to the chin and from the nose to the setting on of the ears. We can also roughly divide the head into three parts: top of skull to eyebrows, eyebrows to tip of nose, and nose to chin. We can, if we like, subdivide these divisions into equal proportions, but it is advisable to keep to the main forms rather than to cut up the face into minute sections which would probably perplex rather than help us.

The student will discover that the faces of men, women and children each need a slightly different treatment, even in rough outline. The inexperienced might start the face of a woman or child with an oval form inclined to the full, but narrowing to the chin. A man's face should be drawn squarer or more blocked in.

Should the model be looking up, the lines will curve upwards. If a straight view, straight lines should be employed, and, if looking down, the lines should be curved downward.

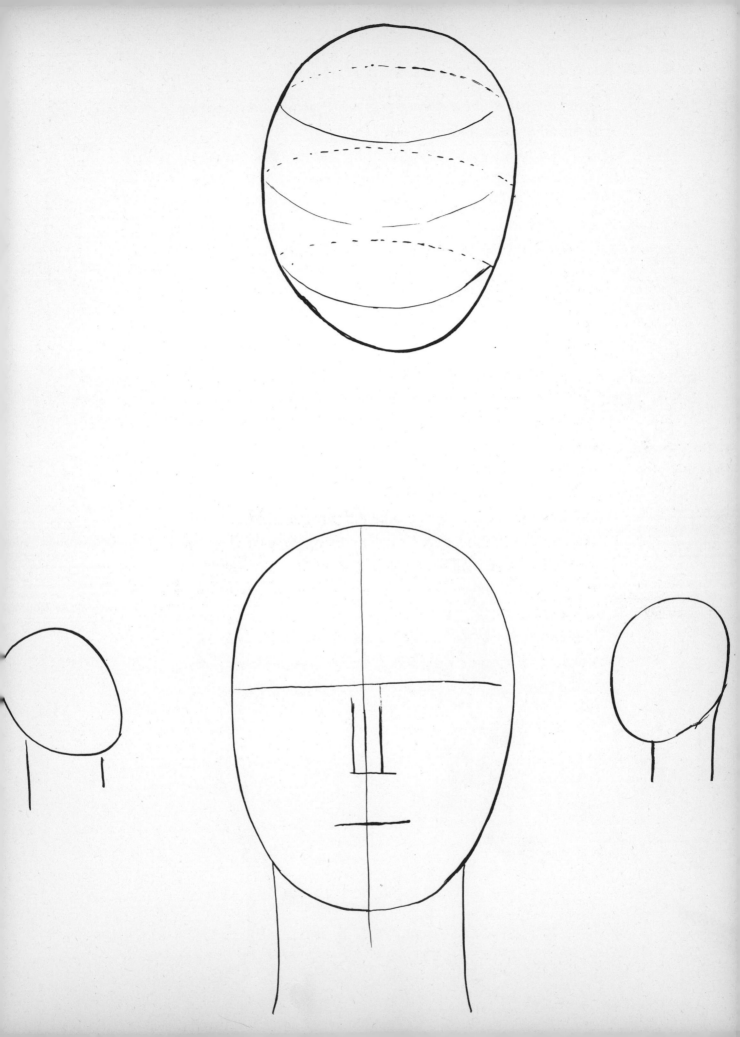

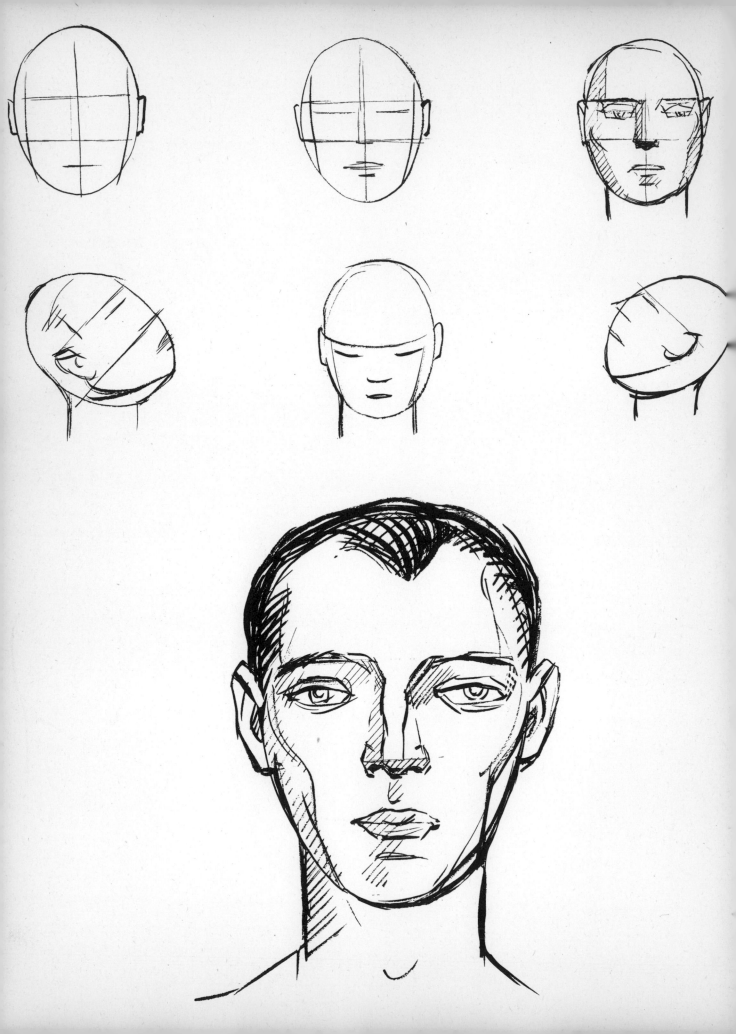

The Neck

In drawing the neck great care must be exercised, for the lines not only attach the head to the body, but they support it and give it its balance. Turn the head as you will, at least one of the two strong cords that stretch from below the ear to the center of the top of the breast bone will bulge out and supplement the outlines of the head. The two cords may be said to form a V that sets, point down, on the top of the breast bone. In this cup rests the head, and as it is lowered or turned, the lines of the cords follow exactly the lines of the cheeks and extend their contours downward.

When the head and neck are seen directly from in front, the cords do not show as part of the outline, but when the body is turned or the head is bent to the side, one will always appear.

The neck and throat too often receive but slight consideration on the part of the student, being treated as though they were other than a distinct form such as the arm or the leg. The firm attachment of the neck to the body at the back is very probably the reason for this. Because of its construction, the neck proper is much shorter in the back than in front. And it should be remembered that the bony structure of the neck is a continuation of the vertebral column and partakes of its supple character, so that the neck shares, to a greater or lesser degree, in whatever action is conveyed by the head. There are, of course,

74

certain individuals who hold the neck rigid with the body and nod the head in greeting, so that all the action will be confined to the junction of head and neck, and this may be in character with the man, but it is not common.

The male neck is short, thick and firm, rising almost vertically from the body, while, on the contrary, in the female the neck is long, slender and graceful, ascending from the body with a greater forward direction.

George T. H. Kerr, whose anatomical studies are used as models by surgeons as well as art students, has an excellent series of neck drawings on exhibition at the British Museum in London. While the Kerr drawings are perhaps too detailed for modern usage, they do prove that almost any portion of the anatomy can be treated in such a manner as to form a decorative and interesting design.

The popular Michelangelo *David* in the Sistine Chapel, sketches of which are observable everywhere, shows another treatment of the neck that is powerful in its delicacy. Of especial interest to the students are fragments and pre-drawings of this great work.

The neck should be seen as a cylindrical column, strong and firm. In profile it descends from behind the ear and the Adam's apple in parallels to the center of the shoulder line.

Men have a larger larynx than either women or children. It protrudes somewhat in front.

The neck moves from side to side and in a rotating motion. It is this rotating motion which allows it to bend forward and backward.

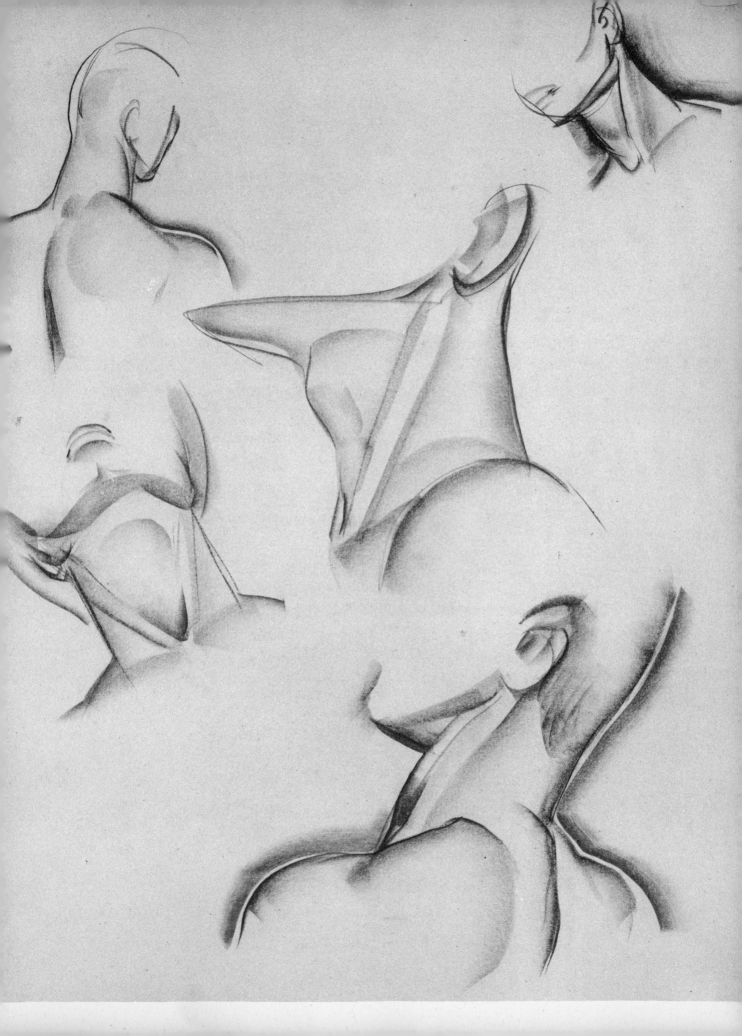

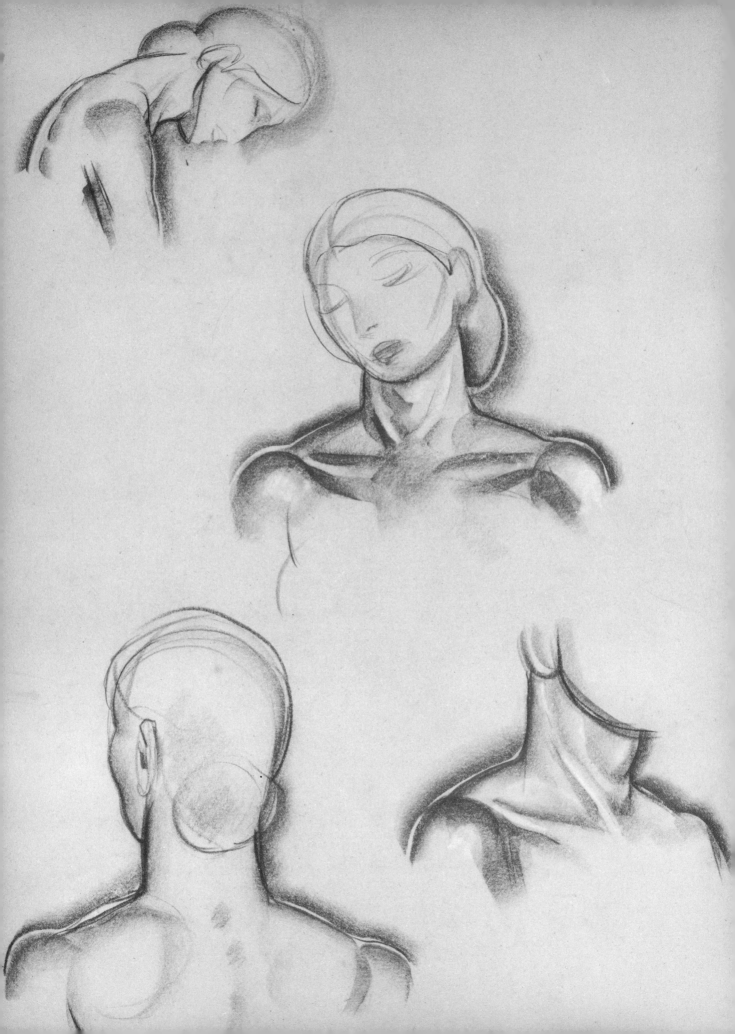

The forms to be stressed in toning the neck are the convex of the Adam's apple and the long mastoid muscle which runs diagonally from behind each ear to the breast bone in the center of the base of the neck. The declivity at the breast bone is triangular in form and is made by the apex of the triangle formed by the long mastoid muscle lines.

But the strong columnar quality must be sought above all; the shading must convey the round form.

The Nose

The nose is shaped like a wedge. Viewed in profile it has a triangular form which normally does not extend beyond the outward oval curve of the face. Seen from the front, the bone of the nose forms a narrow, flat plane as it descends to the tip. There the plane is somewhat wider.

Study the form of the wings of the nostrils and the varied shapes of the nostrils in different individuals.

Much character lies in the shape of the nose, so these general forms are quite variable. However, as construction guides they hold true in all cases.

There is no other feature which so clearly indicates race as does the nose. Negroid, Hebraic, British, Slavic: each has its distinct characteristic. In caricature, where thrift of line is so very important, some artists spend as much time in drawing the nose as they do on the remainder of the face and body.

In portraiture the nose is equally important. Students and critics have learned to recognize the work of the various masters through their individual interpretations of that feature. And, in the case of lesser known artists, periods and countries of origin may be determined. The bridge of the nose, the tip, and the nostrils: all contribute toward characterization.

All that it is necessary to do is to remain faithful to the principle of drawing what one sees.

The noses of different models will vary sufficiently so that there will be very little danger of falling into a pattern. You will not require the services of a professional model in order to sketch the nose. Any park bench or subway car will offer a wide selection of splendid types.

Beware of getting the top of the nose too flat when drawing other than the profile. In the profile the form of the contour of the nose from the frontal bone to the lip is distinctly seen and readily understood, but not so in the other views; the rising and falling of the parts in connection with their increasing and decreasing widths requires some study in order that all the planes may be understood and then expressed.

When the head leans forward, the end of the nose droops down well below the wing of the nostrils, if the action be excessive, and there is no cavity visible; so that in this view we see but the tops and sides, depending upon whether it be a front or three-quarter view. The contour of the nose from the nostrils forward in this view is exactly the same on the two sides, only the reverse of the shape of the under surface when in shadow and seen from below. Note also how the wings of the nostrils slope toward the body of the nose from their base, where they are widest.

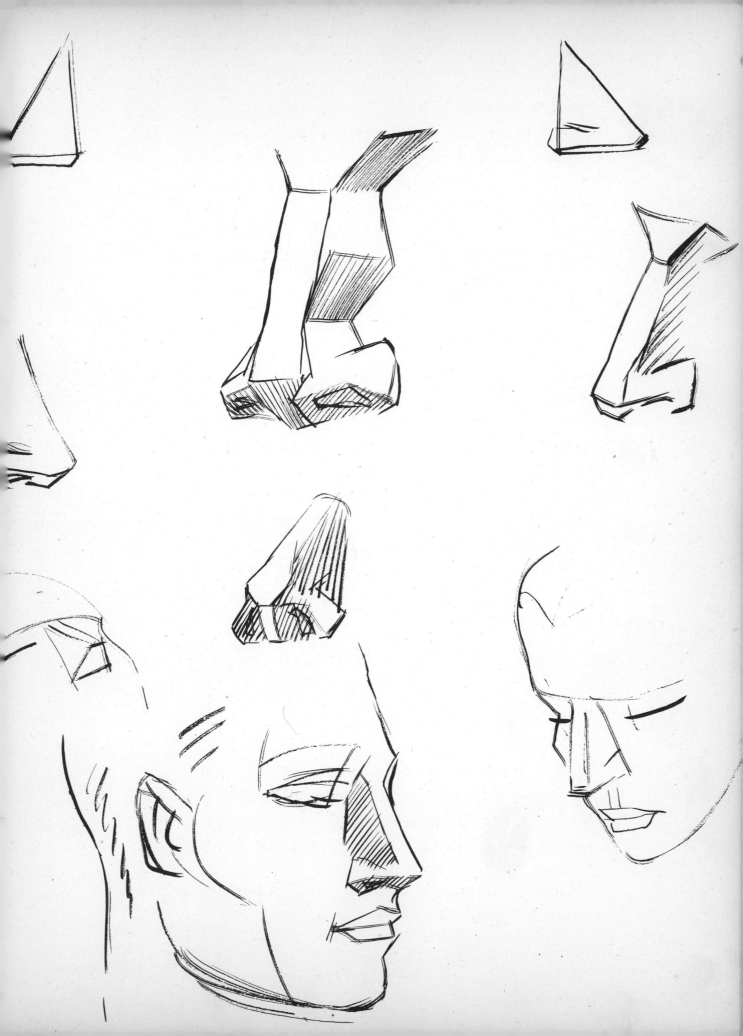

Because of the outstanding position of the nose on the face, its top plane will naturally catch more light and there will be a highlight on the tip. The underturn and the nostrils will consequently lie in deep shadow. From the front view, the sides of the nose will be toned to a lesser degree.

The wings of the nostrils are somewhat subtle in form, but they may be indicated simply with light shadows.

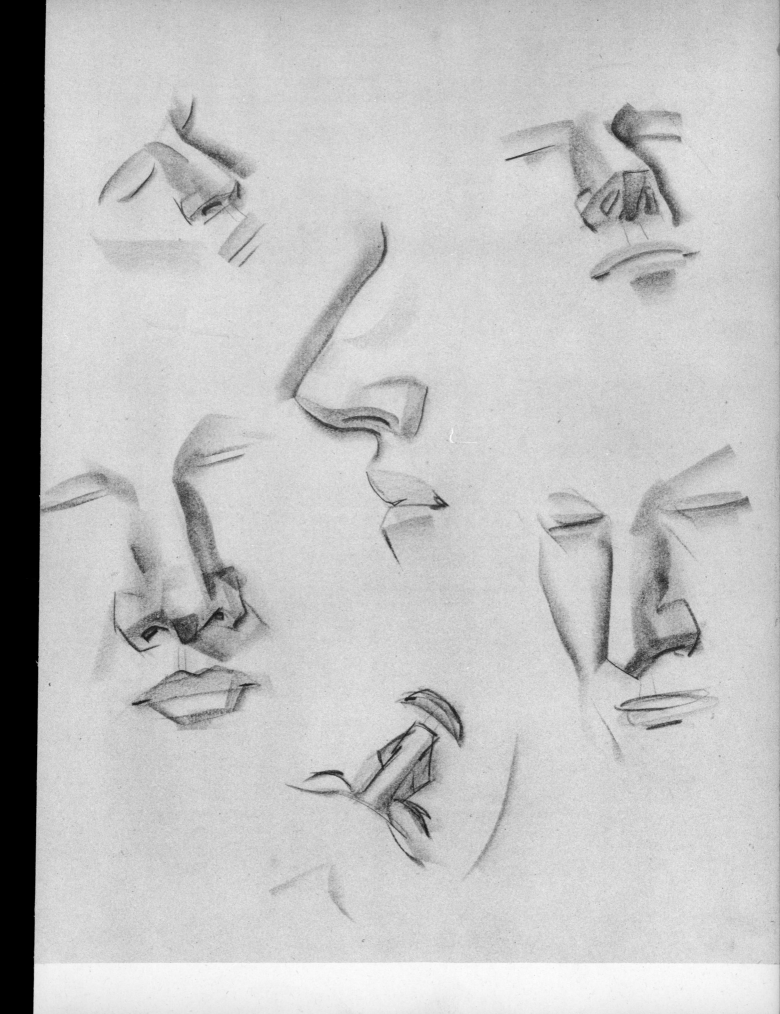

The Eye

The eye is perhaps the most expressive of all the features. By itself it can wink, laugh, frown, weep, express astonishment, anger, love and hate. Love being the most subtle of all the sentiments and hate being the strongest of the passions, these emotions are most marked on the human face.

Cover the eyes of a person and he is unrecognizable to all but those who know him intimately (hence masked burglars). If we can get the character of the eye into our drawing, the portrait is well on the way to success. The eyes and the mouth are the two most changeable and expressive features; therefore we should particularly study them, but it must be remembered that one feature affects that of another, especially in violent passions. The features all work together in expressing the sentiments of the mind. We speak of typical characters or types; we see them in our imagination, and in real life. Living types have been created for us by artists and writers, and from these we form conventions.

For instance, Cruikshank, in his illustrations to Dickens' works, and Charles Keene, in his *Punch* drawings, have given us types which we cannot better, and Shakespeare and other geniuses have conceived, in words, good and bad characters from which we have founded our conceptions.

The poet, the actor, the cleric, all have their special attri-

86

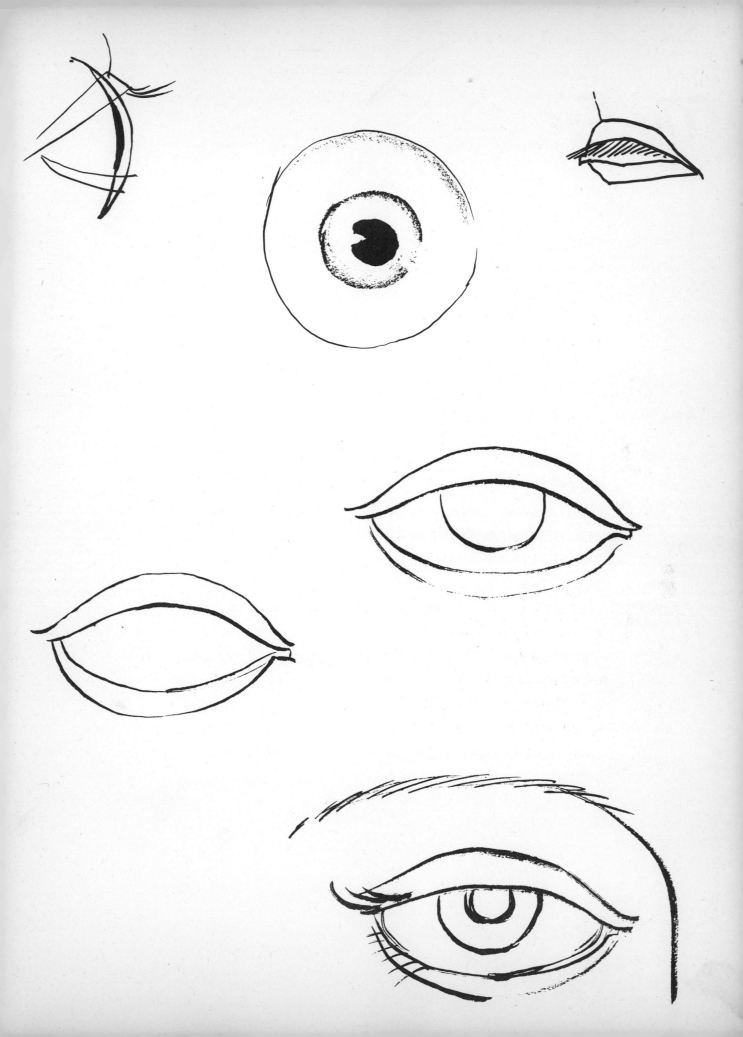

butes in look and gesture, conventions which we mentally follow when representing such personages. This we see in every profession and in every nationality, with the possible exception of the Oriental, who cultivates an expression of stolid indifference and control over his emotions, seldom disclosing his thoughts through his expression, his countenance to the western mind being blank and expressionless.

In drawing the eye, the main difficulty is to place it correctly. However, if the masses of the forehead, cheeks and nose are seen properly, the placing of the eye becomes automatic and will not go astray.

Here is an analysis of the main features of the eye proper, but you will do well to remember that the eyebrow and the forms immediately surrounding the eye are of equal importance in drawing the eye correctly. The distance between the eyes is, as we have said in our chapter on the face, about equal to the width of one eye. The upper lid overlaps the iris slightly. Always be certain that both eyes are focused properly.

In the half-tone drawings you will notice that the eye is actually formed more by the shadows around it than by its own outlines.

After you have acquired and digested these general axioms of placement and construction, remember that in the eye, to a greater degree than in any other feature, is to be found the mood intended to be conveyed. The partial or complete lowering of the lids, the widening of the eyes, the raising of one eyebrow; any of these results in an entire change of expression.

Study the eye in action and purpose, rather than in too much mechanical detail.

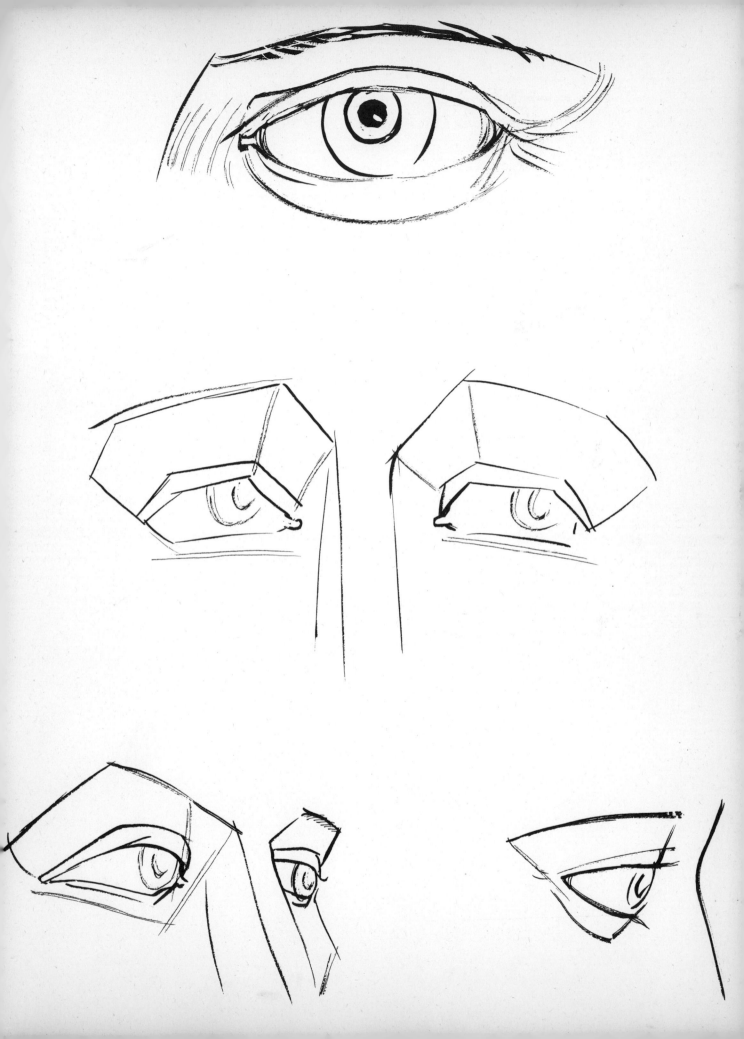

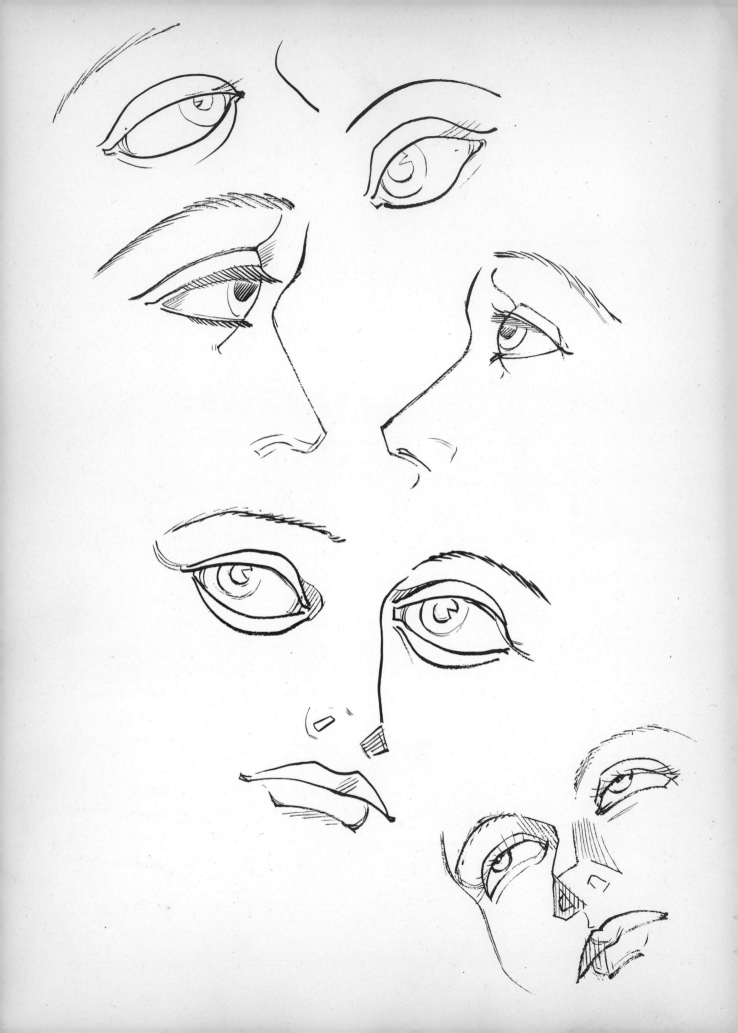

Though these shaded drawings retain all the features of the line studies of the eye, observe how they show the curve and turn of the forms to much better advantage. This is because the "value" or intensity of the shaded forms bring out certain portions of the eye, throw back others.

The side of the nose forms a wall which throws a strong shadow, covering the inner corner of the eye. The outer corner curves toward the cheekbone, thus acquiring a shadow in the front view. These two shadows serve to emphasize the roundness of the eye and the curve of the retina.

The Mouth

There can be no imagination without memory. The brain of the artist, if he is a figure draughtsman, must be stored to the full with every detail of the human form and its actions before he can invent or revisualize on paper what he may have seen years before. Gustave Doré shows this great faculty in his black and white illustrations, for memory and imagination are inseparable one from the other.

The fundamental part of the art student's education is practice in drawing. Memory for color follows later. No artist can draw what he has seen definitely and artistically, still less can he color or truthfully record with pencil or brush, unless he can formulate the image in his mind. Let the mind be brought to bear on the subject, and so learn its fundamental principles, before the hand commits itself. Those who study art possess an immeasurable advantage over other people because of their increased appreciation of Nature, with its endless incidents of life and movement. It is an artistic privilege, augmented by a good memory, and is not shared by the inartistic.

Leonardo da Vinci writes, in his *Treatise,* of studying in the dark, on first waking in the morning, and before going to sleep, "I have experienced no small benefit, when in the dark and in bed, by retracing in my mind the outlines of those forms which I had previously studied, particularly such as had ap-

peared the most difficult to comprehend and retain. By this method they will be confirmed and treasured up in the memory."

Of course da Vinci was not always so entirely right. In his same *Treatise* a curious misstatement is made regarding the knee joint. He says: "Of all the members which have pliable joints, the knee is the only one that lessens in the bending, and becomes larger by extension." And again, "All the joints of the human body become larger by bending, except that of the leg." We have only to measure our own knee when in these two positions to see that exactly the opposite is true.

These apparent digressions are not so far-fetched as they may at first seem. Drawing is, after all, something more than

putting lines on paper. Every aspiring artist must have some understanding about method as well as execution.

Perhaps the above paragraphs will help the student realize that the mouth is never to be drawn as a slit. It is a concrete mass superimposed upon the face. The fullness and roll of the lips should be examined and their forms brought down to the simplest terms. You will notice that men's lips do not differ very greatly from those of women, except in size. Avoid the puerile "rosebud" and the ridiculous "cupid's-bow" in drawing a woman's mouth.

From a front view, you will notice that the corners of the lips are farther back than the middle portion. This results from the curvature of the teeth. It is through a proper usage of the corners of the mouth that you will express the desired mood. Except when fixed in a broad smile or a laugh, the major portion of the lips remain virtually unchanged in character. By drooping or raising the corners of the lips an infinite variety of expressions can be indicated.

The student will do well to utilize the popular conception of characterization through depicting the several types of lip construction. It is of course not quite true that lip formation is necessarily a key to character; yet for purposes of symbolic portraiture it serves a definite objective. Thick, sensuous lips are used to portray moral looseness or weakness; the thin straight line is indicative of self-righteousness, the stuff of which fanatics are made; a wide mouth denotes generosity. Whether or not these generally accepted ideas are actually true should not concern the artist too greatly; the sole fact that they *are* accepted will facilitate his characterization to no slight degree.

94

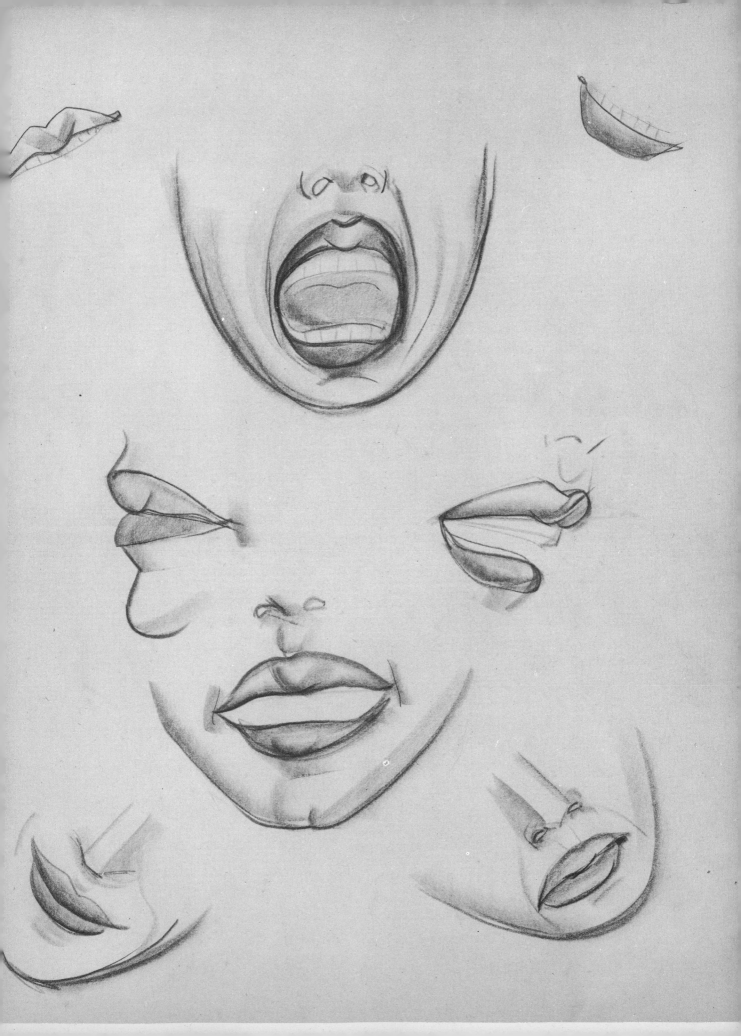

The Ear

The ear is apt to be neglected by artists for several reasons. The first of these is the ear's retired location. Second, the ear is often hidden by the hair and headdress. And finally, the ear takes no part in the expression or action of the head. The draughtsman, however, is readily betrayed through his neglect and it is in just such forms as the ear that he shows his skill and knowledge, and the beauty and delicacy as well as the strength of its intricate forms are worthy of his most careful attention.

But it is not necessary to construct the ear as though it were an intricate plan for the communications of a great city. Without ignoring its fundamental features, the organ may be conceived simply and with force.

If the ear is well placed there is rarely any difficulty in connecting the head with the rest of the body, for it is easy to imagine that all lines that do not follow the curves of the outside of the head pass inward and terminate at the ear. It is like a railroad center, with numerous tracks running in from all directions.

All lines point toward the ear, such as the curve over the back, the curve of the throat, the line of the jaw, the line of the hair at the temple, and sometimes even the lines of the eyelashes, eyebrows and mouth.

Practically all the best models of dressing the hair, particu-

96

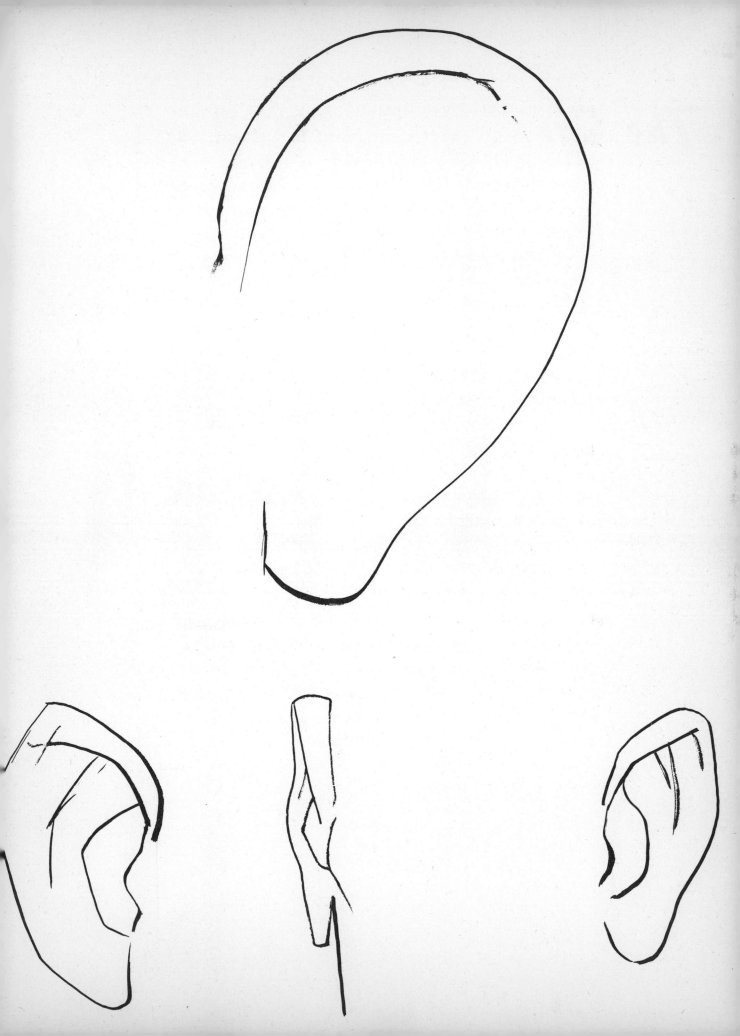

larly the Greek, have lines running to the ear as a basis of their decorative design. More than this, the ear is a fixed point, like the hub of a wheel around which revolve the spokes, for, when the head is tipped forward or backward, the ear acts as a pivot. The position varies with the individual, but its lowest point is usually about opposite the base of the nose, and, if of ordinary size, the top is about opposite the eyes, which, as we have said, are always half way up in the whole space of the head.

The irregular shape of the ear makes a generalization of form somewhat difficult to arrive at. The greater part of the ear is like a shallow bowl with a turned-out lip that runs around the outer edge. The lobe forms a small loop at the lower end of the ear.

Do not spend too much time on the convolutions which make the inner part of the ear seem complicated. The hollow which leads to the drum and the little flap of skin where the ear joins the cheek will be all that you need indicate in order to draw a simple ear.

The ear lies horizontally between the lines of the brow and the tip of the nose. Viewed from profile, it lies in the middle of the head.

Naturally, occasions will arise when you shall deem it advisable to alter the position of the ear for purposes of realism or design. If this should be the case, do not hesitate to do so. Del Sarto and da Vinci did it frequently, Michelangelo more often than not. You will be in excellent company.

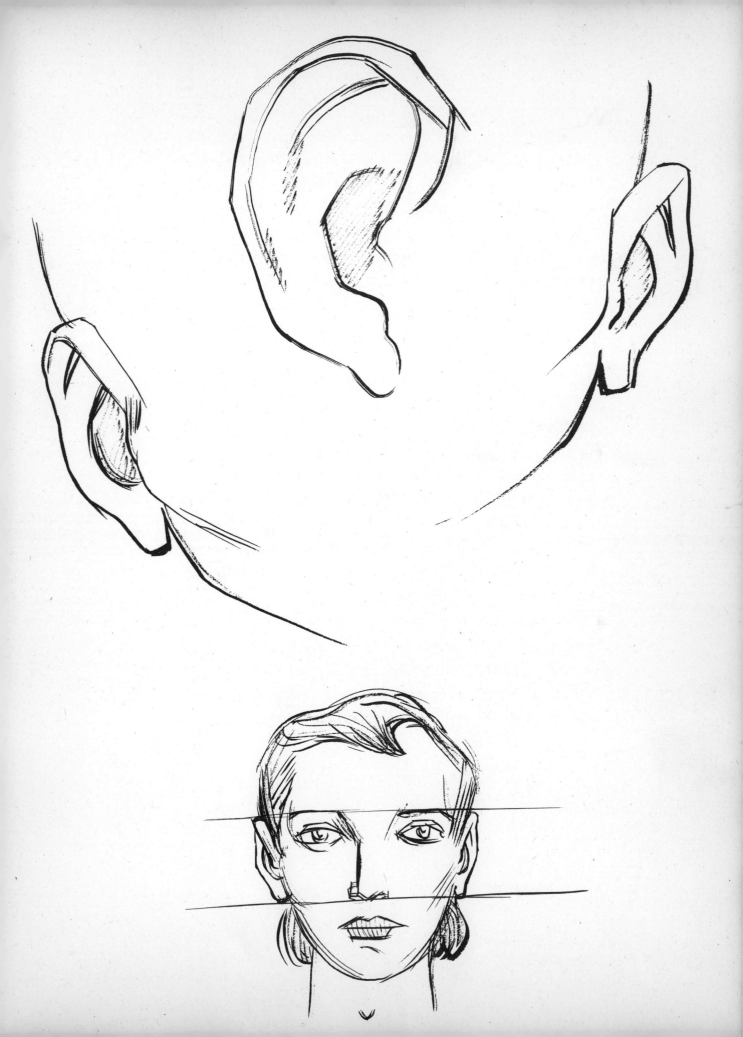

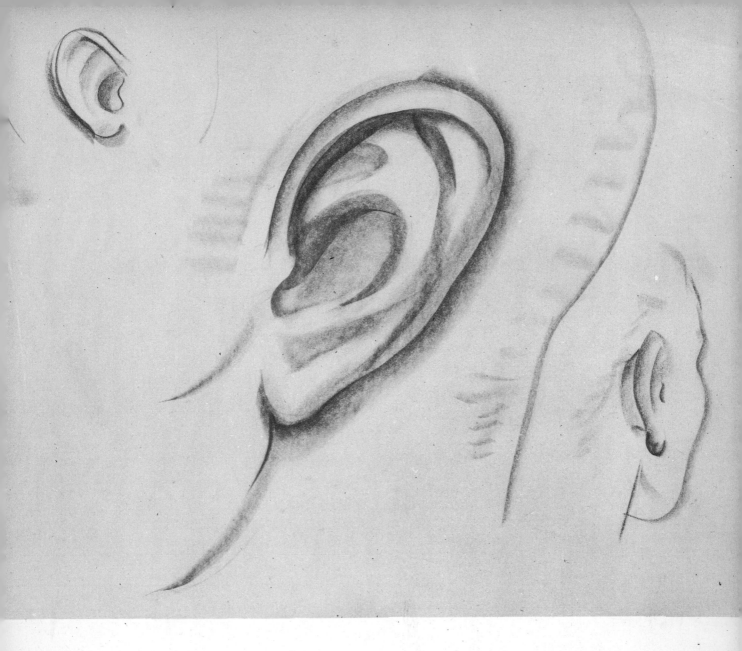

In the shaded ear, the deepest tones will be at the ear drum, under the edge of the rim which circles almost the entire form, and at the point of junction of the lobe with the jawbone. The secondary convolutions deserve study for their more subtle tones.

101

The Female Torso

There is a drawing by Michelangelo in the British Museum, probably a study for the marble Torso in the Vatican, which is a rapid sketch made up entirely of convex curves. It looks right because the great draughtsman knew exactly which points to emphasize, as in the collarbone and the knee joints. Throughout its rhythmic flow it shows no angles or straight lines. But only a master draughtsman could get a similar result by the same methods. Again, it is doubtful if any artist of modern times was more a master of pure lines than Ingres. He had an absorbing love for what he was trying to represent on paper, and his outline was the perfection of meticulous correctness. No man had a more penetrating eye for following a curve along its course.

When the artist has gained experience he can get away from this triteness and adopt a less mechanical line, but he should not let it worry him if his line at the first attempt is incorrect so long as he sees his mistakes. He should not rub out but should try again, as his next attempt, helped by the incorrect line, may be right.

With difficult or subtle curves we must try several times before we find the right form, but we should never force or put down our lines too firmly until we are certain. In this respect we have a great precedent to follow in the drawings of Michel-

102

angelo and other great draughtsmen, who felt their way by leading and helping lines. It is far better to make mistakes in the footsteps of these great artists than to have the cocksure, mechanical ability sometimes found in lesser artists, with the certainty of being right the first shot. You can learn far more from the mistakes you make than from mechanical correctness. If you look at the drawings of Alfred Stevens or Kathleen Kaye, you will see traces everywhere of their feeling for, and finding, their lines.

Miss Kaye's group of figures in the heoric canvas, *Women of Athens,* shows more regard for line value and draughtsmanship than is perceptible in most paintings. Despite the strength of the torsoes depicted, the observer cannot help but feel the natural inclination and the curving delicacy of the lines. This outstanding quality is very probably caused by the fact that the artist was already a proficient draughtsman before she entertained any idea of painting in oil, a condition which is only too often lacking with so many of our present-day painters.

The female torso, as it is used today, differs greatly from the typical female torso as exemplified in *The Archers* by Michelangelo or almost any group by Raphael. The modern female torso is narrow and small, the waist longer and more flexible than that of the male.

A woman flexes the upper part of the spine most in bending, a man the lower part.

The shaded female torso brings out the body's soft grace. The forms of the shadows must be pliant and not so definitely defined as in the male. The deep tone between the breasts and the modulating tone lines to the wide hips are the accentuated points of the shaded torso.

The Breast

In the female figure the line of the breasts must follow the movement of the line of the shoulders. Do not place the breast too high, although in drawing youthful figures a small, high breast emphasizes their youthfulness.

The breasts are not centered, but are placed somewhat toward each side and point outward. When the arm is raised or lowered, the breast on the side of that arm must follow the movement, as is shown on the following plate. Should weight be placed upon one arm, the shoulder is thrust up and the muscle by which the breast it attached is pulled upward also.

The breast of the female is like a half sphere with a slight tendency toward the conical, due to the raised nipple. The breast does not lie upon the front of the body, as we have said, but in a measure upon both side and front horizontally, and upon the ribs vertically, so that being placed from front to side the female breasts point away from each other.

The base of the breast thus conforms to the contour of the form upon which it rests. When the figure is fore-shortened this is particularly noticeable. However, in drawing the breast be guided by the character of your model, for we shall soon see that there can be no hard and fast rules concerning the shape or formation of the breast, depending upon racial type and heritage.

110

There has never been one standard type of beauty or ideal in the female breast. Different nations have idealized different developments, just as different nations have different preferences in food, clothing and modes of living. Whether these ideals were promulgated by desire or by the stock on hand, we may not be positive. It is more reasonable to assume that the latter is perhaps the correct surmise. Changing times and fashions had their voice in the matter, too.

The German nations have been fairly consistent with a rounded highly-placed breast. The Italian is lower and more bulbous. In many periods of French history women's breasts were made to appear almost spherical. The American ideal is modeled after the Greeks of antiquity—small and firm. The African is more pointed.

Powerful emotions may be depicted through an understanding transposition of the female breast. Manfredi's *Messalina,* in the Louvre, has this quality to a very great degree. In the painting all the facial features are blurred; the torso, the legs and the arms are swathed in some gauzy material. Only the breasts stand out bold and clear. Yet the observer senses the evil and feels the might that is latent in the great spheres.

112

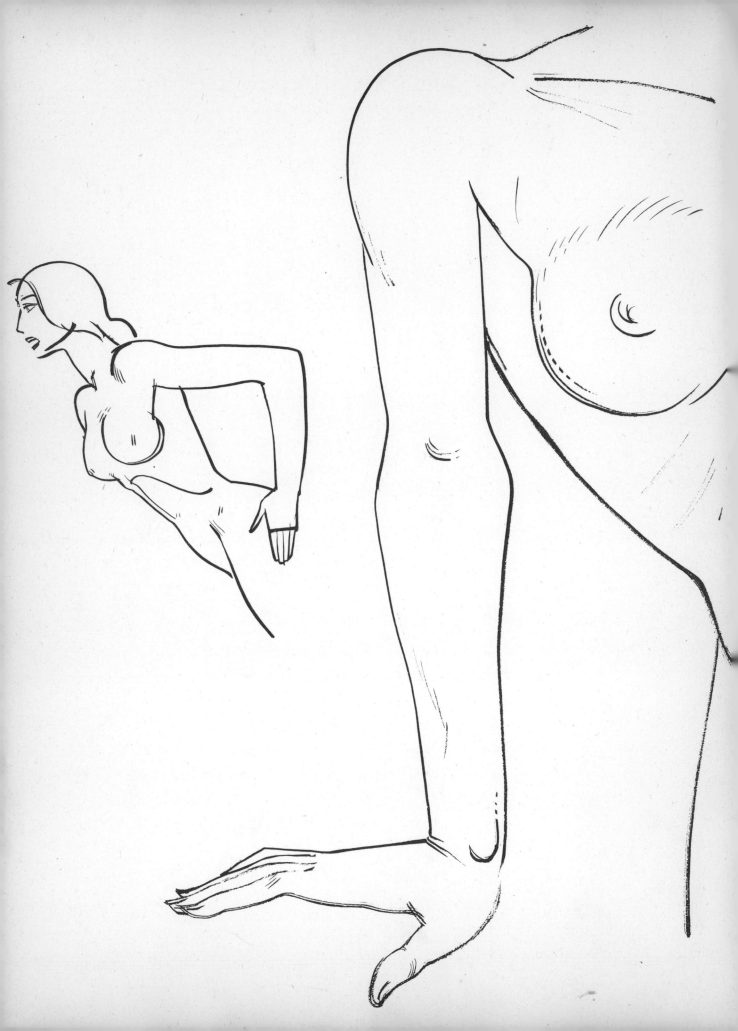

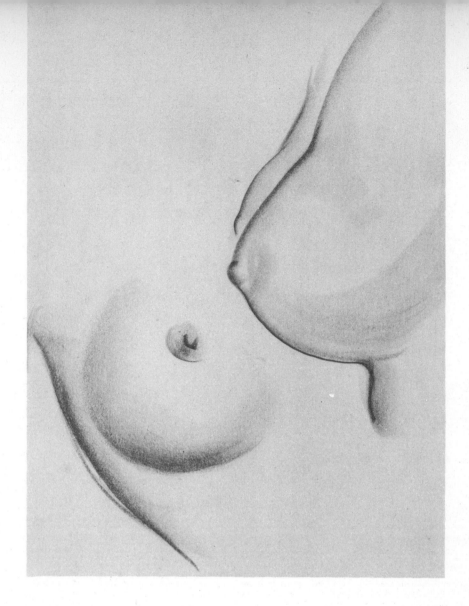

The base of the breast forms the contour, and, as in an inverted bowl, it will be there that the shadow will lie. The intensity of light and the direction of its course affects every shadow form, but in normal light a deep shadow gives the line of the lower edge of the breast where it lies on the rib cage.

The deep valley between the breasts must be expressed by tone. The highest point of the breast will have the highest light. This point is close to the nipple. The nipple is toned because of its color value.

The Pelvis

Outline is a convention, founded largely upon imagination, for a border line does not actually exist in nature. Once again we refer to da Vinci's *Treatise,* where it is written: "The knowledge of the outline is of most consequence, and yet may be acquired to a great certainty by dint of study, as the outlines of the different parts of the human figure, particularly those which do not bend, are invariably the same. But the knowledge of the situation, quality, and quantity of shadows, being infinite, requires the most extensive study."

Everything we see is composed of masses, of shapes, of color, with varying effects of light and shade. There is no continuous line of demarcation, for everything blends, almost imperceptibly, except where a light mass comes against a dark, or vice versa, when there is a definite edge to the parts of the object at which we may be looking. Notwithstanding this fact, we find that the simplest and most direct way of representing each form is by outline alone, and this convention, as we know, has been practised from time immemorial. It is the basis of all good design and the groundwork of all knowledge of form. We must learn the simplest means of representing fundamental facts before contemplating the more complex problems of light and shade. The artist can express his artistic sensibility, his feeling for form, in pure line more obviously than by chia-

116

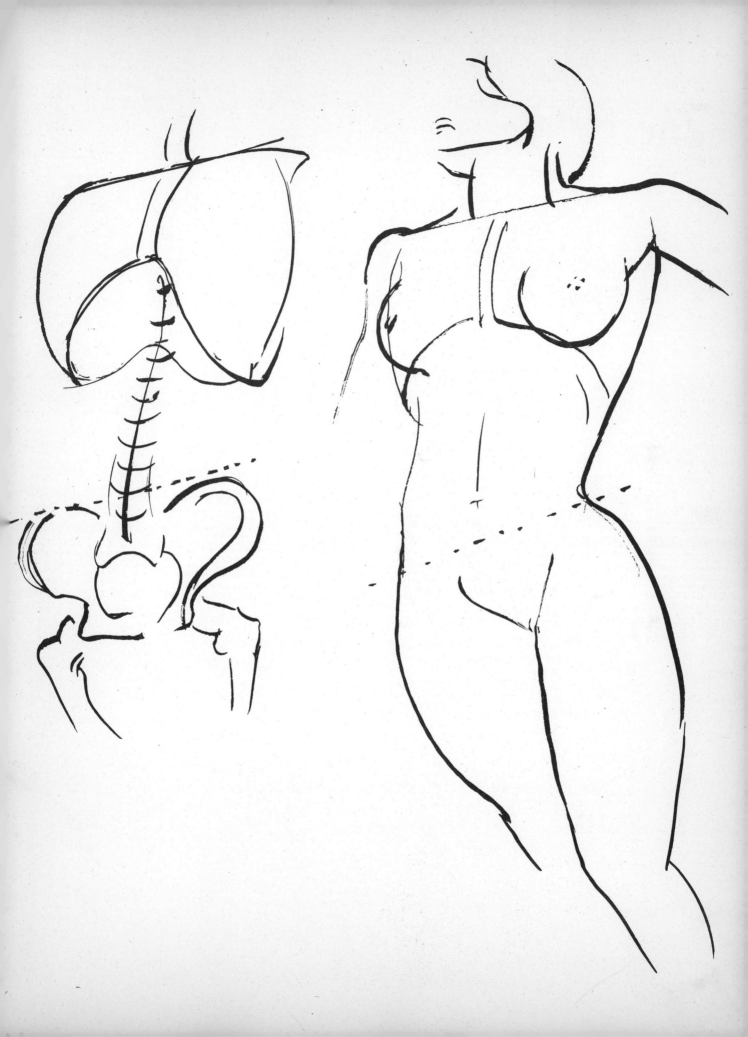

roscuro. No two artists put down a line in the same manner. Their personalities come out of their finger-tips, directed by their brains. That is the reason why the drawings and sketches by the best of the Old Masters are so varied and vital.

In figure studies, the line should be as long as possible and not patched together, but it should vary in its feeling and pressure according to whether the flesh or bone is being represented. Some young students, under the mistaken impression that they are getting "style" or vigor, affect a cocksure, broad, black outline for their nude studies, composed entirely of curves, thus emphasizing their faulty drawing—the same line serving for the joints and hard surfaces as for the fleshy parts.

Scale should also be taken into account, for a thick or heavy outline which might be right in a large drawing would look out of proportion in a small one.

The wedging in of the lower part of the body between the buttresslike hips forms the most notable instance of the interrelation of parts in the human organism. From this region emanate all the important actions of the human body, for the hip and the pelvis form the point of transmission, from lower to upper part of the body, of all the power that controls movement.

To understand the human form it must be drawn from many points of view. This will enable the student to see form as the sculptor does, so that he will see around his view, and conceive the idea of solidity without the sacrifice of silhouette.

Now, the function of the pelvis is to support the mass of the abdomen. The direction taken by the line of the hips and the pelvis is the clue to the pose of the figure. When making your drawing, determine their position at the very beginning.

118

Female Figures

There follow fifteen plates of the female nude figure. Some are in action, some in repose.

The first plate gives merely the skeleton, to show the wide pelvis and the hip bone—they are both considerably wider than in the male figure. The rib cage, spinal cord and skull formation are worth examining for simple structure, framework knowledge.

The other plates show the method of shading the delicate forms and contours of the female nude. Forms are outlined in nearly a monotone, with accentuation at only a few points. The background is toned in, as no shaded figure should be drawn against the dead white of the paper. No such lighting exists in nature; therefore you should not attempt it. Notice that part of the modeling of the drawings is achieved through using the background.

When the student has the opportunity, he should make notes of those muscles which come into play under action, and those that are relaxed when the model is in repose. What is lost by relaxation of the body is balanced by those muscles which are extended. For instance, a man walking must have the balance or center of gravity upon the foot on the ground, but this is not so in running when, owing to loss of equipoise, the center of gravity is lost, and the more this is lost the greater will be the action. In running quickly, the balance is lost and recovered by almost instantaneous movements, which the eye cannot follow entirely but which must be understood. Slow motion films show us this.

A concentrated and comprehensive vision is essential in seeing the whole object at once, and this is only possible with the figure at a sufficient distance from the observer, both in regard to its proportions and to its general unity.

Our first aim in quick poses is to see the figure in contour, with the inner modeling suggested by a few salient touches indicating the bones and prominent muscles, which will be sufficient to give solidity to the figure—a fact which should be ever present in the memory, for form is the prime essential in drawing the figure nude or clothed.

Always search for form, never losing sight of the figure in its entirety. Separate parts should not be regarded too intimately until the whole figure unites with ease. Labored lines can never well express vitality or movement; the more momentary the action, the more economy and freedom in the line. The quicker we draw the better, so long as we keep up the tension of our eyes, brain, and hand, all working in unison. Not only must the eyes see, but the mind must comprehend.

"Accuracy of form and modeling must be learnt before quickness of execution can be acquired."—Leonardo da Vinci.

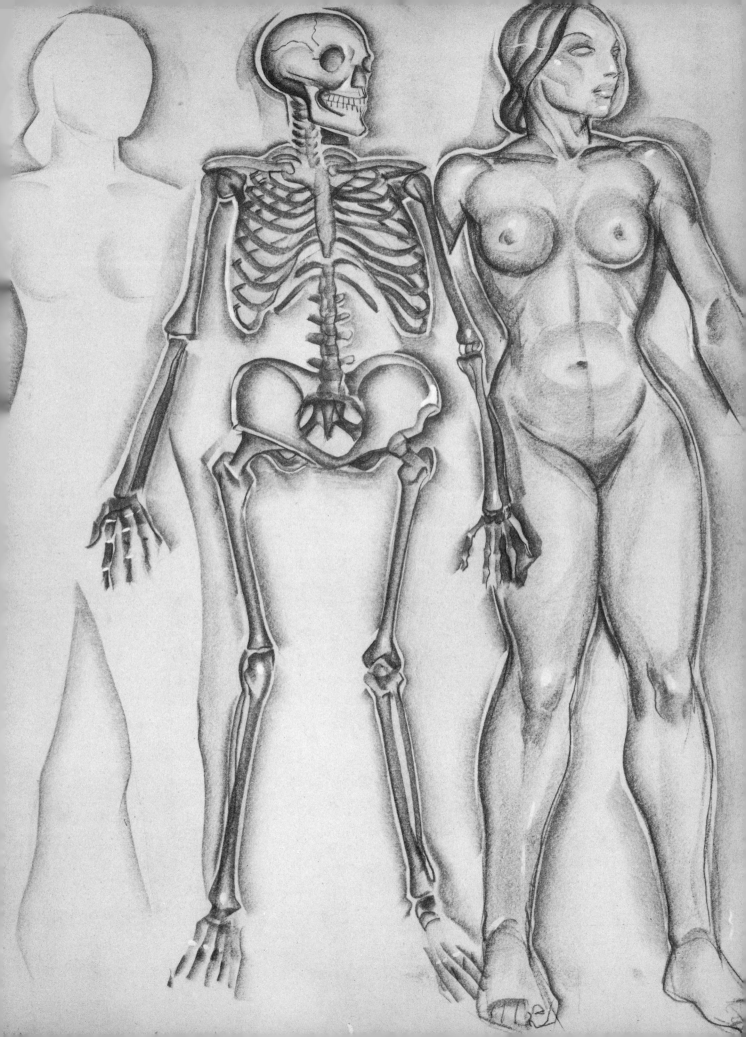

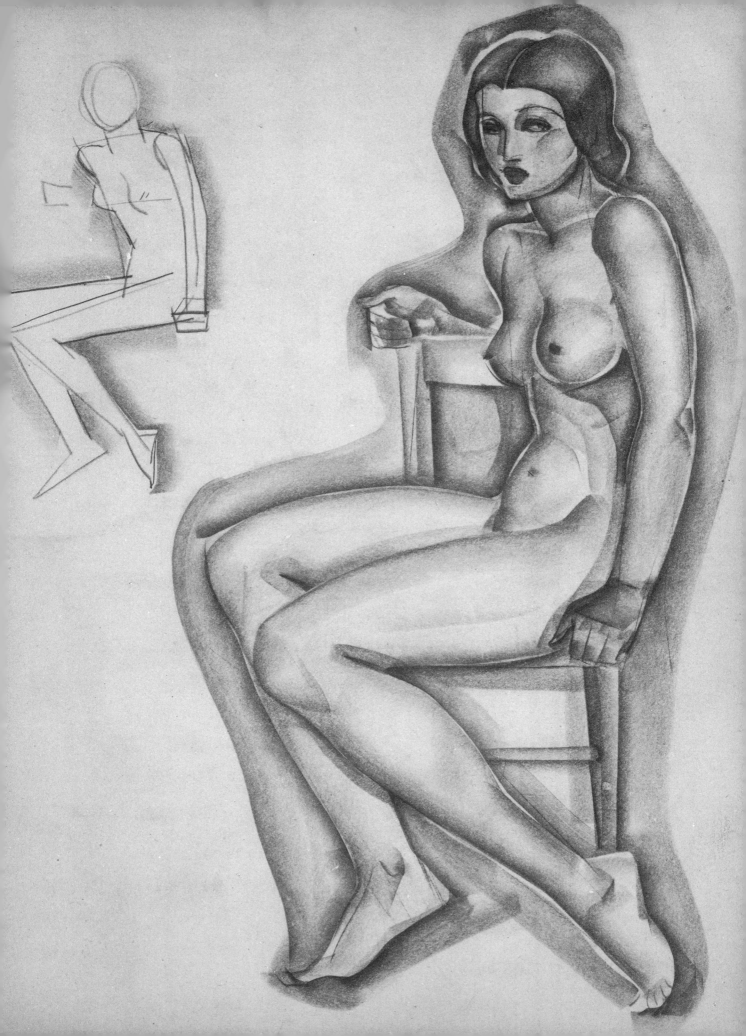

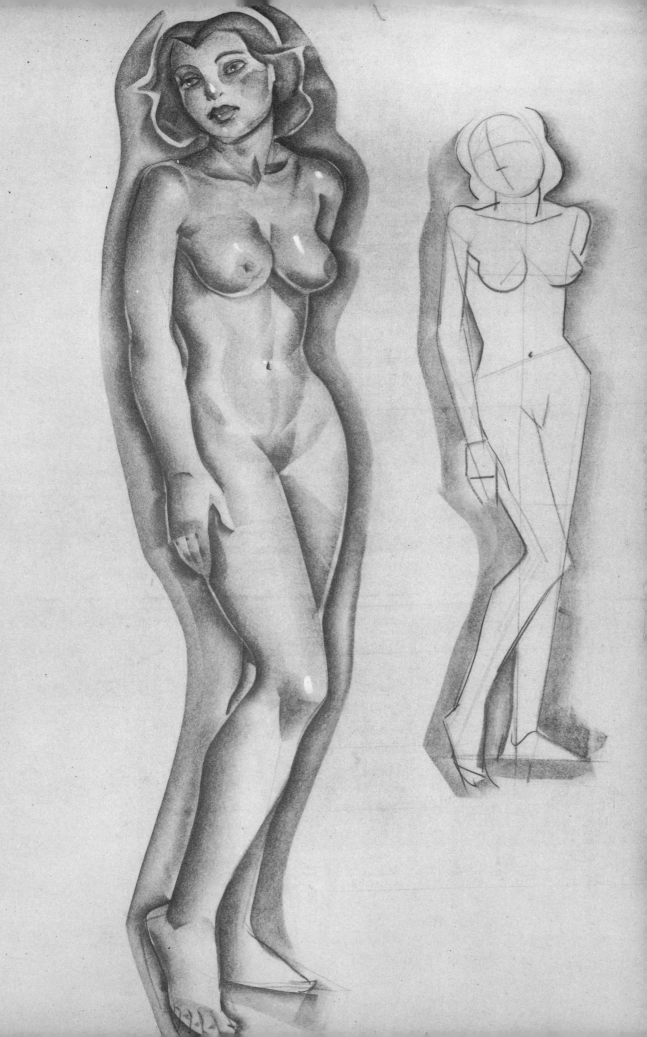

Action

Walking and running action is a series of falls and recoveries. The extent to which a figure is thrown out of balance indicates the speed of the motion. The difference between the two actions, walking and running, is not shown only in the position of the legs but in the increased action of the arms, the forward thrust of the head, and the strain of all the muscles. The two figures on the following plate demonstrate the essentials in drawing these actions.

The relative height of the feet should be very carefully studied. Failure to place them correctly in relation to each other will change the perspective, hence the action.

Experience will show that there are times when the action of the whole figure is helped by the absence or omission of certain outside lines. However, a drawing must have a synthetic quality and a power of suggestion to seem complete without being actually finished.

You must be a clever artist to be capable of portraying vividly in a few moments a figure in complex action, with a minimum of lines put down directly from life or from memory. There are some draughtsmen who have this enviable gift, but who are at sea when, with the nude figure before them, they attempt to make a finished drawing. Then they seem to become paralyzed, or tentative in their lines, and draw in a

half-hearted way. Such an artist resembles a musician who can play by ear but not from notes. He has quick observation and a retentive memory, but the artist who can draw from life has a sounder knowledge and a more scholarly outlook.

It is useless to draw a figure in motion until the law of correct balance, and the loss of balance, is well understood. Applied to a drawing, when it is successful, it is more expressive than any amount of detail, and gives all that is needful. If the action is intense, it is advisable, if possible, always to draw the figure in the nude first.

The direct line is the more difficult, and can be successful only if the artist feels at his best and is keenly alive to what he is doing. To see economy of line, the student should carefully study the drawings by Rembrandt, Forain, and many clever contemporaries. A thorough knowledge of the figure is essential if one is to draw successfully in this manner.

In the simple action of walking, viewing the figure in direct profile, we find at the start that a vertical line, dropped from the nape of the neck, will divide the figure in equal parts, the line falling between the legs at equal distances between the left foot and the right, the latter flat on the ground and the former slightly raised, with the right knee bent.

At the first movements of progression, we find the equilibrium still sustained, but with the feet wider apart, the left heel more raised and the right touching the ground, the left leg more bent until the right heel comes direct in a straight line with the nape of the neck. Then the left leg is gradually brought forward with the knee bent until it straightens, and the action becomes the same but is reversed to the left, as at

140

commencement. Up to this point the right arm hangs vertically beside the body. The left arm swings gradually forward, then backward, as the right arm comes in front. On completion of the motion, we notice that the left foot is firmly planted on the ground, the right set well back with toes pointing downwards, knee bent, and the vertical line touching the nape of the neck and the right knee. Throughout all these changes the body will always be upright, with the head slightly bent forward. Both in front and back views the vertical line will fall from the pit of the neck through the navel, and between the feet, or between the shoulder blades and heels.

In the more violent action of running, the arms, at the start, are extended into an almost horizontal position, with the body and thighs well bent forward, the front knee under the nape of the neck, the feet well apart. After these first few instantaneous movements, rapid changes take place which the eye cannot follow, but both arms drop, the thighs are thrown forward, legs well bent with right foot off the ground, the left leg straightened with its toes touching the ground in an oblique line, with the body and right foot off the ground with knee well forward in a vertical line with the head. The next change is that the right arm swings back and the left is brought forward, and so on, until the reverse movements take place, the right leg going backwards with the left forward, gaining in rapidity during progression. The equilibrium is much the same as in walking, but more frequently and rapidly lost and recovered. Throughout this action we notice that the muscles of the legs and thighs are tense, and the body in an oblique or forward direction.

Shading, as well as line, helps to convey action, and movement tends to eliminate the opportunity for the observance of detail. Long tone lines to show the stress and strain of moving muscles and changing planes will give increased speed and beauty of motion.

Male Figures

The following plates show the execution of quick studies, twenty-minute poses. The object was to bring out power and lithe strength in a few strong lines and tones. Some of the sketches may seem to have been carried quite far, nearly "finished," but this effect can be achieved by covering the toned areas evenly and working out a pattern of muscles. Maximum power is attained by stressing the long muscles.

In drawing a portrait of a man or woman we should note, and seize upon, a characteristic attitude before we begin our work. A scientifically arranged picture is seldom quite natural or instantaneous in its conception, however beautiful it may be in line or rhythm. An instance may be given of the Bridgwater *Madonna and Child* by Raphael, a picture which, with its suave line and perfect rhythm, rivets the attention of the beholder. Here is art in its greatest beauty. But is the child quite natural? Have we ever seen an infant take, of its own accord, quite so affectedly beautiful a pose, conforming with the lines of its mother? Lovely as it is, this is a picture arranged according to traditional rules and principles, as so many of the pictures by the Old Masters were, though, of course, some of their finest conceptions were composed without thought of rule, their genius and their keen sense of symmetry carrying them along into a creation of perfect balance and rhythmic beauty.

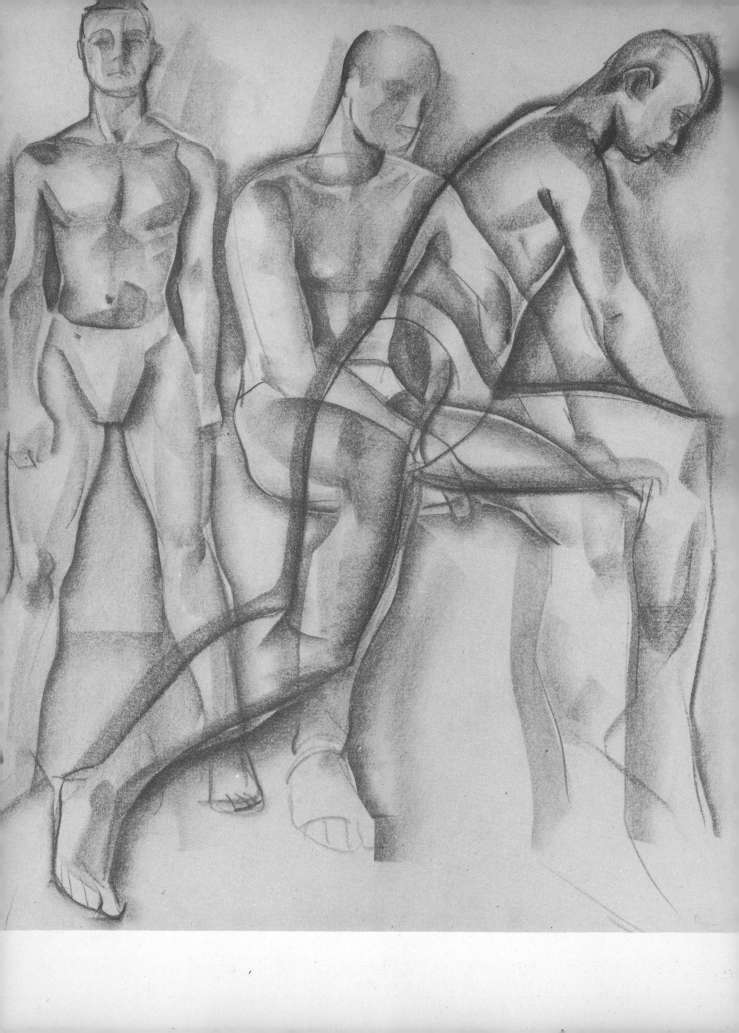

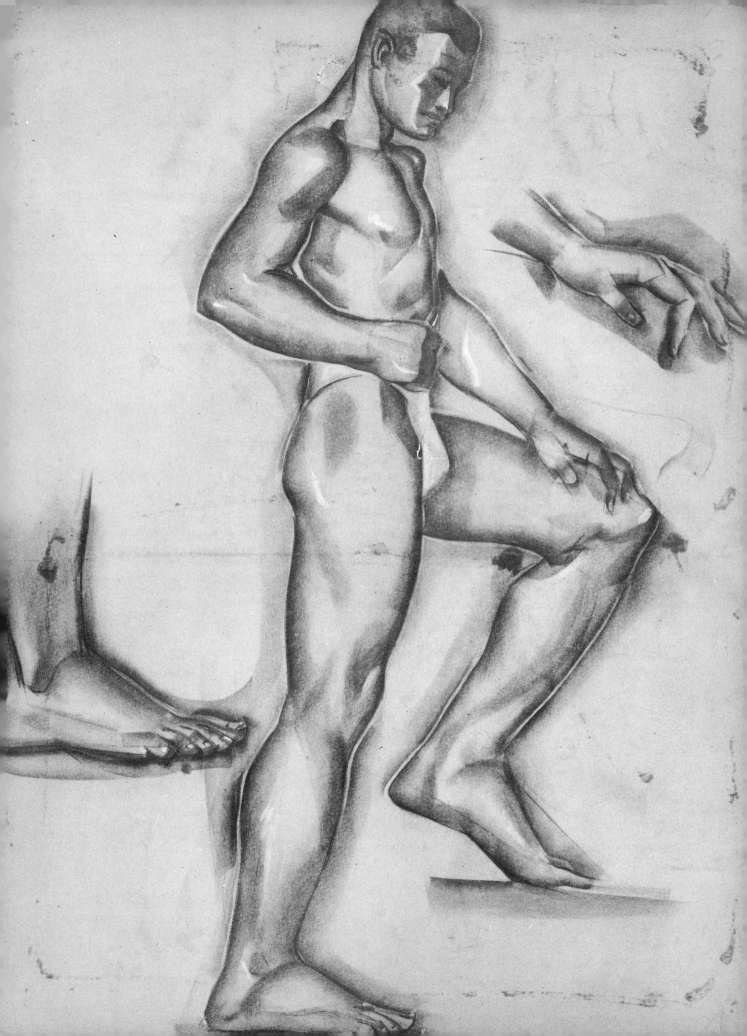

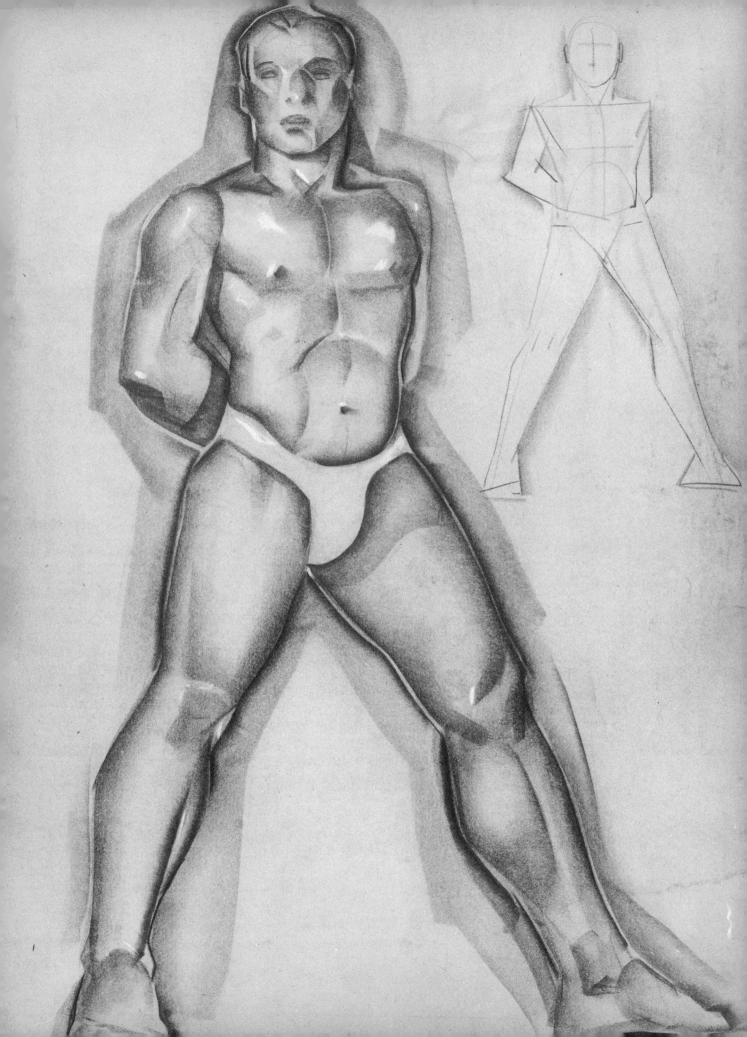

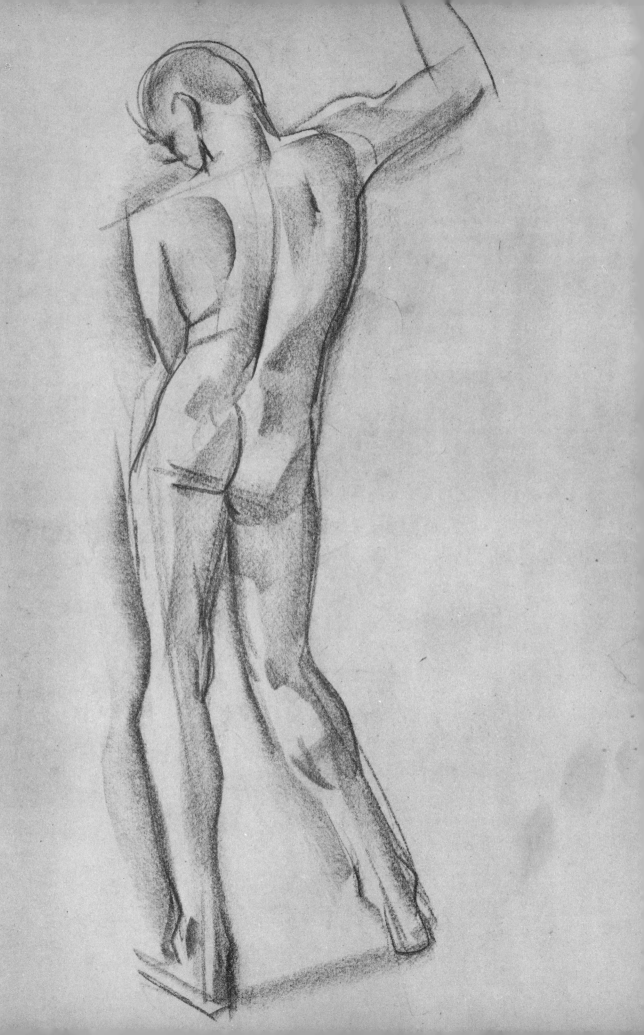

The Clothed Figure

After you have learned to draw the nude figure of the female with reasonable accuracy, it is a fairly simple matter to superimpose a costume upon your drawing. In the following plates you will see the nude figure, then the same figure clothed. The clothed drawing is virtually a drawing of the nude with the sleeve, neck and skirt line added.

The average artist will do well to avoid imitating the usual fashion drawings in the execution of his clothed figures. Even a brief glance will prove that these pictured mannequins do not in any way resemble live women. Anatomically they are all wrong. It is doubtful if a woman shaped in that way could really live, let alone walk, eat or balance herself.

Anyone who has so much as glanced at the figures adorning the pages of our fashion magazines or at the advertisements currently appearing in the daily papers, will understand the truth of that statement. The legs are slender and long beyond belief, as are the arms and the throat. Heads are minute, features stylized almost to extinction, hands overly fragile, and the feet would fail to carry even a very small woman's weight.

But, however different from the human form these figures may appear, it is well to remember that they do serve a very definite purpose. And even the most individualistic of fashion artists had first to learn the fundamentals of the actual human

162

figure. Then, with these principles mastered, he was able to go on and develop his own method of fashion drawing.

In drawing the clothed figure, our first consideration is the correct movement of the limbs appropriate to the particular action, and to make certain that all parts hang well together. This necessitates an acquaintance with the various joints and muscles of the extremities and limbs. The head must be well set upon the shoulders.

Should the limbs be foreshortened, those creases at the joints will be more in evidence than in other parts, and this is where some knowledge of anatomy proves useful. We often see draped figures drawn with an excess of folds, or, worse still, with folds in the wrong place. François Millet, in his picture of peasants, shows how admirably he understood this fact.

Rapid outline sketches of such subjects will be found most useful for future reference. There can be little time for blocking in the figure when the model is walking or in rapid motion, and the best one can do is to sketch in the complete form as quickly as possible with a few lines and omitting detail, depending upon memory to fill in the smaller parts. Summarize your figure and fix the proportions in your mind in a flash, before you begin it, for the first rapid impression is generally the true one. After all, a few faults of proportion in such notes are not of much importance if we get the right spirit of the thing.

164

The clothed male figure presents a somewhat different problem from that of the female. As the trousers and coat do not follow the lines of the figure as closely as a dress, their cut and drape must be studied. Their heavy material gives them a structural identity of their own, and only at points of stress does the figure reveal itself.

The following seated figure (in shirt sleeves) shows how you must conventionalize the clothes forms simply, just as you did with the anatomical forms. The plate with the skeleton reveals how few points of contact the protruding bones of the body had with this clothing.

Well-worn clothes, such as a laborer's, partake more of the form of the body than new ones. The chief lines and folds of the clothing indicate the attitude of the figure, as, for instance, the bagginess at the knees in men accustomed to much digging and agricultural labor.

In cities, the clothes of men do not adhere to the contours of the figure, although the variations on this theme are very probably as numerous as the tailors and clothiers in each town. Different styles and fashions must be applied in different manners, too.

The texture of the cloth may be brought out in various ways, depending upon the medium used. Each artist will develop his own methods of doing this, using his brushes, pencils, etc., in a manner best adapted to his particular style.

This will introduce a series of drawings which show the male and female figure in various poses: some in action, others in repose. Study the figures to learn the action of the clothes in different positions. Notice, too, how they are affected by the

167

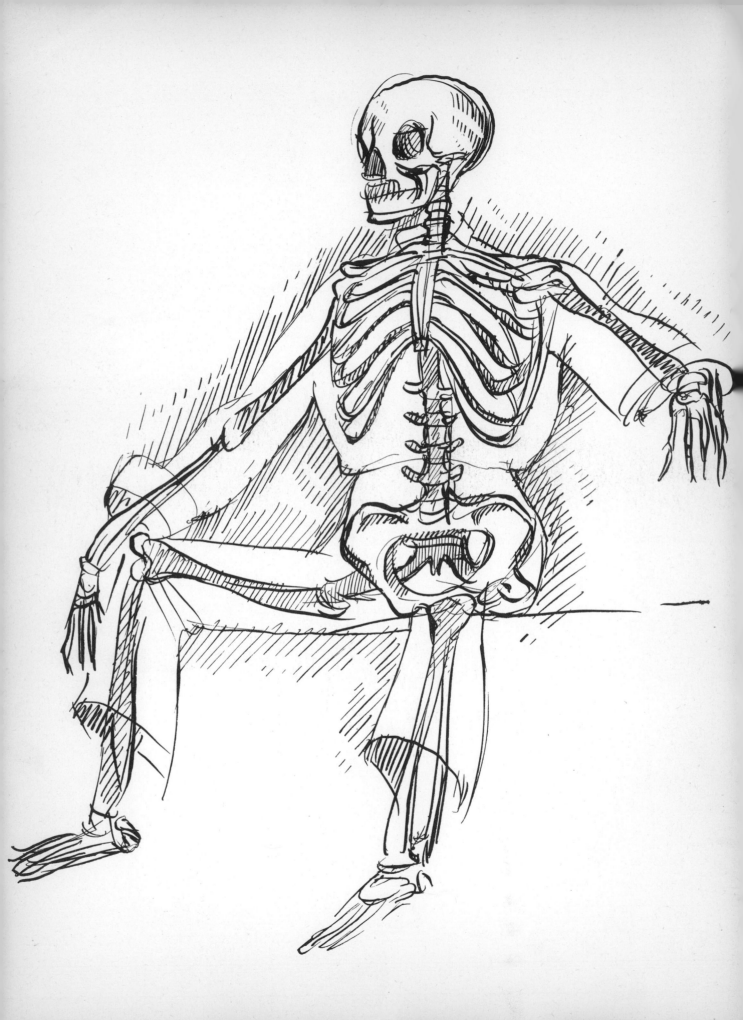

movement of a leg or an arm, the bending of the waist, etc.

In the case of each female figure, the clothes were super-imposed upon the nude. The males were treated in the manner heretofore described. Here again you will find the absence of unnecessary detail, simple forms being adequate, perhaps preferable, for our purpose.

The folds and creases in clothes take many changes in different positions and movements, but only those that are essential should be marked, the less important ones being omitted, as a superabundance of folds is a bad fault.

Draperies should show by their outlines the movement or attitude of the body and limbs beneath. An angular tendency is preferable to a too-rounded or curved representation. One may learn a great deal from the drawings of Adolph Menzel, for the hang and fit of the clothes on his figures was always right. His illustrations for *Frederick the Great* are excellent examples.

Some very fine artists show a tendency to ignore the details of modern dress, patterning the clothing of their models after the simple line of beauty which was the Greek ideal. This plan does not mean that these artists drew their subjects wearing the Greek tunic; it means simply that they blended the clothing with the functional design of the body.

170

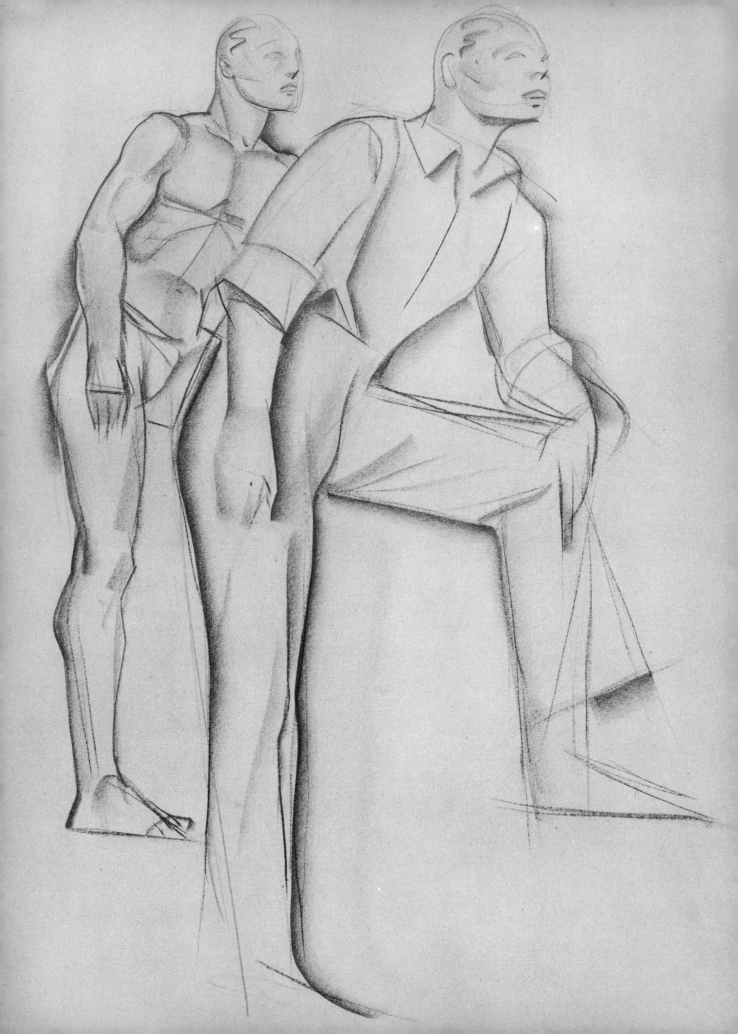

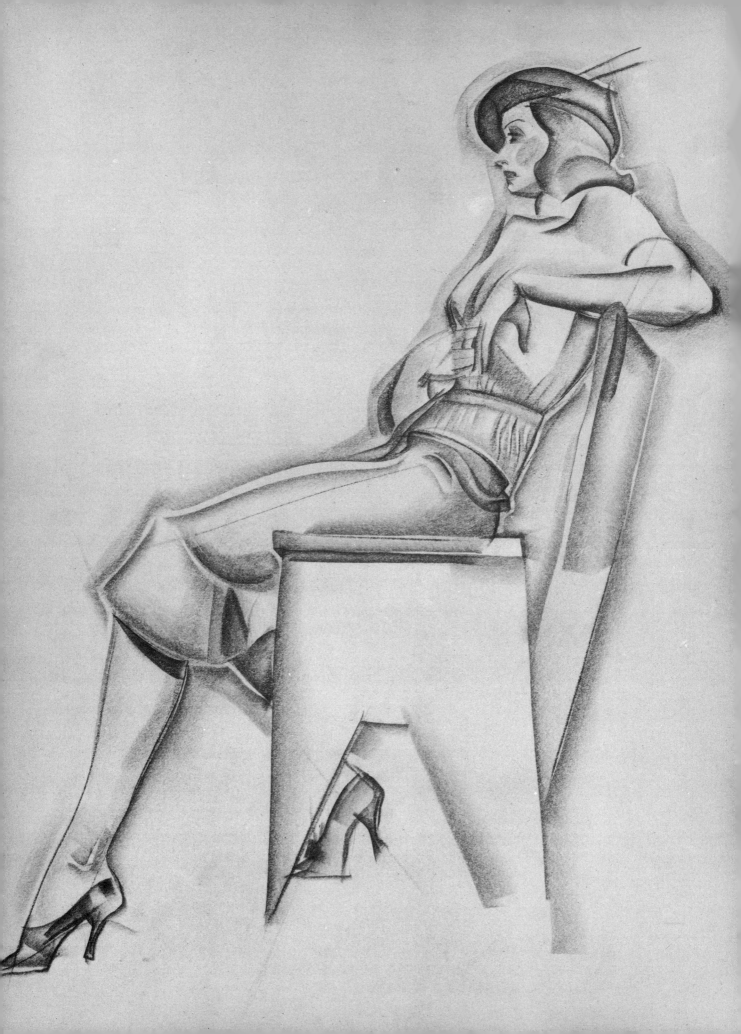

Repose

The reclining figures on the next page show how the force of gravity will cause one side of the entire body to become a base line; all the other lines of the body will follow toward that line within the limits of their anatomical possibilities. In order to get the maximum "repose" quality in your drawing, you will find it necessary to stress, perhaps exaggerate, this natural bodily tendency.

A sitting figure is considered difficult to draw because of the short lengths into which the long lines are broken. In this apparent confusion, however, there is always a structural order that may be based on convex and concave curves.

When drawing reposing figures, facial lines and features should correspond accordingly. In that way you will be able to convey your whole meaning in its entirety. If the face and the figure fail to correspond, the net result will be confusing in its direction.

In seeking to convey a first impression aspect much that is unnecessary has to be left out, and such detail as is considered essential must be concentrated in the right place.

Art is largely a matter of imagination, elimination and selection. It remains for each individual to determine the direction of his particular bent. There are, of course, two sides to every discussion, and we have no desire to be identified with any specific cause. To our way of thinking, there is much to be said for both schools of artistic thought: each in its own way contains merit and fault.

There are those who claim that art, in order to be true, must be photographic. And this statement is a thorn in the side of those others, equally sincere, who prefer abstract art, or "impressions" of nature. We think it entirely possible for the two schools, in theory widely separated, to meet on a common ground in practice.

One thing should be understood. In every piece of work there is some message that the artist is trying to convey. However, if people will not look at a drawing, or if they are unable to understand it when they do look, then that particular message has been lost.

Despite the lack of action, a figure in repose does not preclude the possibility of conveying such a message. Perhaps the message may be more subtle, but it is there nevertheless. The quality of repose may be transmitted in various ways, but the final effect is always the same. For that reason the lines employed must differ in value from those used to denote action. Sometimes these differences may be reduced to extremely simple terms. One very clever craftsman has stressed vertical lines in his action sketches, while in his reposing figures the horizontal lines stand out.

196

Even in sleep, few people actually rest all their muscles—
many remain tense, with clenched fists, strained face muscles
or taut thigh muscles.

The artist must try to convey complete relaxation by undula-
ting line and rhythmic design and shading. There must be no
sharp, upthrusting angles to disturb the action of gravity on the
resting figure.

Beauty is a term that has never been quite accurately defined. Its meaning must be wide enough to embrace not only beauty of form, color and effect, but artistic expression in the rendering, with technical perfection of workmanship. Most students with training can draw a face or a figure more or less correctly as far as mechanical measurements can make it so, but that is not drawing in its true sense, for it tells nothing beyond hard facts. When students have mastered this science, art comes in, and the artist can express himself as he pleases, with a sure foundation of facts to support him. Apart from imagination, art is more elimination than enumeration.

The pre-Raphaelites, by the poetry of their imagination, made their art greater than they did with their literal representation, which was more or less mechanical. What made Ingres' pencil drawings fine? The wonderful appreciation of beauty of line, the touch, the sensitiveness for rhythmic flow, with the accents unfailingly in the right place, perfect characterization and impeccable draughtsmanship. What made Michelangelo's drawings much greater? Passion, power, knowledge, and himself. And Whistler? Perfect taste with an exquisite delicacy of touch, and the art of selection.

The next two plates are drypoints executed with a diamond point on a copper plate.

The attitude of repose is intensified by attempting to get laxity into the lines of the reclining figures. One rigid, unpliant line will counteract all the effect created.

THE SISTERS. A dry point—executed with a
steel needle which throws up a burr that catches
ink; warm and soft tones are thus created

SIESTA. A dry point

Grouped Figures

In composing a drawing of several figures we should not rely too much on rules and formulae. An agreeable pattern, with a not too conventional design, is what we have to aim at. It is the artistic sense that enables us to give expression to what we think will come well in the arrangement of our composition in black and white. This does not apply to painting, for color entails more thought and consideration, and there are perhaps greater difficulties in front of the artist.

Originality in art is cultivated from observation of the truths and facts of nature. A well-stored memory will enable him instinctively to put his drawing together in a pleasing and natural order.

The marvellous pen and ink drawings of Daniel Vierge are recommended for study. His illustrations to "Pablo de Segova" are, perhaps, the most remarkable technical compositions in this medium that exist. Vierge's drawings are well known to many figure draughtsmen, but are practically unknown to the general public. They are all amazing compositions, unsurpassable in their knowledge of light and shade, action and form.

Some modern artists seem to care little about natural compositions, but strive to appear original by imitating what has been done in ages past by primitive man—Byzantine and Ancient Eastern Art—plagiarism of the worst kind, for what was created originally in all seriousness of purpose is often distorted into mere eccentricity, with a view to cheap notoriety and self-advertisement. These perpetrations lead to no advancement on the primitive art of early days, and ignore what was a natural evolution from the first crude efforts up to the present day. Such drawings are only commonplace repetition, lacking all soul and deep intention.

On the other hand, there are many contemporary and "modern" painters who pursue an independent course, and pay little heed to old traditions. They follow their own imaginations and instincts in their outlook, perhaps at their best adding another chapter to the evolution of art—a very healthy influence on the cheap sentimentality and shoddy commercialism of which we have had too much, especially during the Victorian Era.

In the first eight plates which follow, the models' poses have been worked together to form simple compositions. Do this with your model (and try to have a model as often as possible). Pose the model twenty minutes in each position and draw them directly into your groups. Do not mind the overlapping lines showing through—you can clean them out if you wish, but avoid erasing: not only because it makes your work look messy, but because one gets to rely too much on rubbing out instead of putting in.

You will find composing-as-you-sketch excellent training in placing figures for more serious compositions.

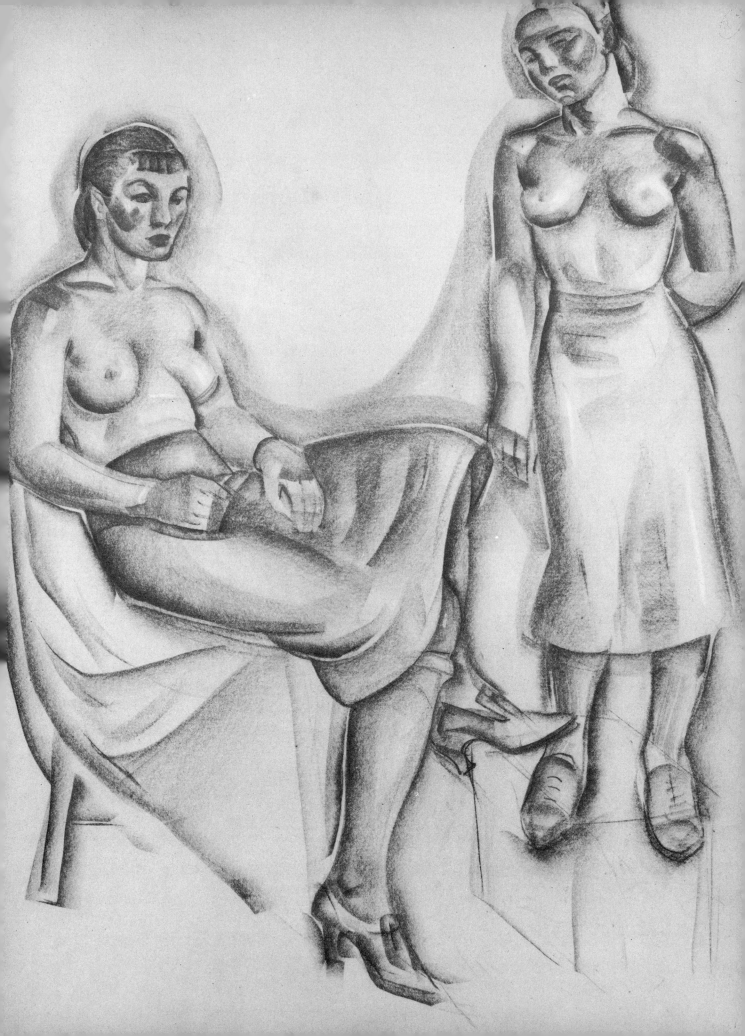

Back and Side Studies

The balance and quantities of line and mass all go to form a good design. That the artist is working to rules must not be too apparent, but in a figure composition each person should have a distinct motive, and there should be a real reason for his being in the picture. There must be unity and purpose throughout the work, and what the artist has to say should be said forcibly. Each object should fit in with its surroundings. Each figure should have decided character.

Any pictorial representation, whether on paper or on canvas, must of necessity be caged in by its dimensions. This of itself compels the draughtsman to present what he has to say within a given space, and he must avoid the appearance of having had to bunch his figures together to fit within the limits of his drawing. The effect we should give is that of plenty of room to move, not obviously or unnaturally composed.

The next group of plates are a series of shaded drawings which show the back and side views. These studies will serve to bring out an analysis of back forms and show how they may be carried out in line drawings to appear finished, without yielding the simple essentials and bigness.

Each muscle and plane that appears in these shaded drawings was put in for the purpose of showing the "intention" of the pose; i.e., to accentuate the essence of the model's action.

212

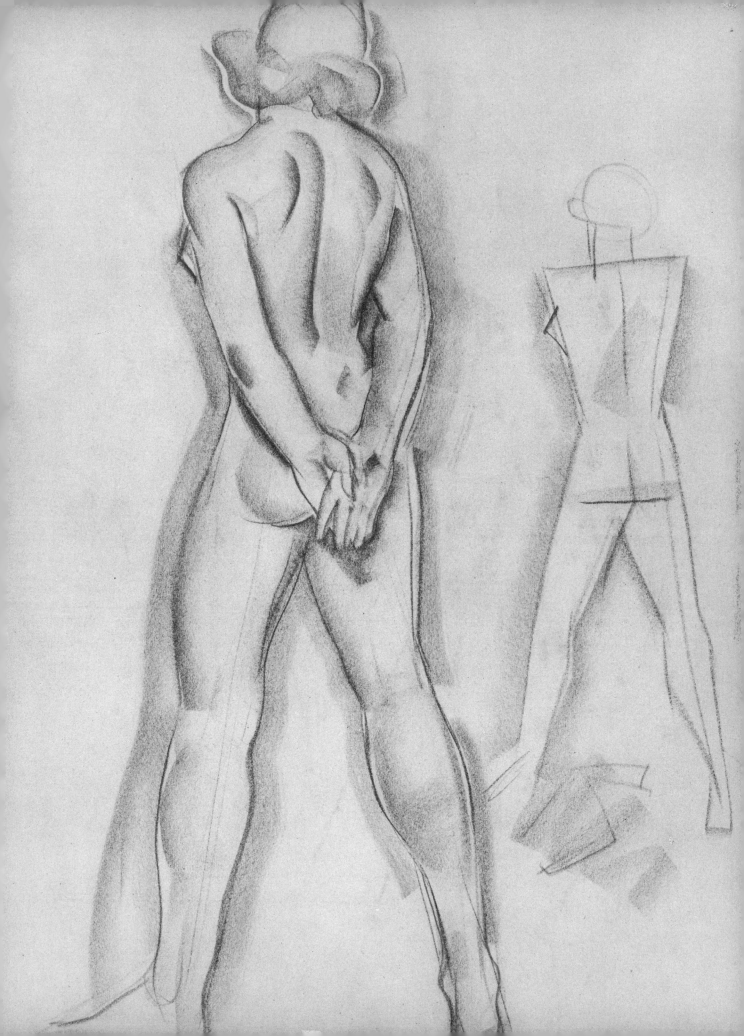

6957.

Shading

Pencil, chalk and charcoal possess peculiar qualities of their own, and each one is capable of different treatments. The lead pencil, if managed well, is in itself beautiful in both tone and texture, and is, perhaps, the general favorite black and white instrument. It is the handiest and most useful medium for all general purposes, and especially adaptable for sketching out of doors, figures, landscapes, and architecture; while for portraiture it is unrivaled for beauty of quality. It is certainly the most difficult of the three mediums to manage really well, but with practice the artist can achieve and express every shade and texture that he needs, providing he has suitable paper, responsive and sympathetic to his touch.

In suggesting the use of Conté crayon or any other lithographic crayon for sketching and shading, the purpose is not to teach you "tricks" or "techniques", but to facilitate a quick rendering of even tones. In order to cover a large area in charcoal or pencil, long and considerable application is necessary.

One can use the side of the Conté crayon very effectively for sketching in tone. In order to edge a line, merely exert more pressure on the edge—still using the side of the crayon. Practice with this beautiful medium will develop your individual approach.

The last few halftone plates of this series on shading are

221

heads in varied light. Notice how the accentuation of a tone can be used for increasing the expression of power in the face, as in the man before the crucifix and in the man on the plate immediately following.

The white highlight around the head is achieved by bringing the background only to within an eighth of an inch from the drawing, using the side of the crayon to get an even tone. It helps give an "air" to the drawing and there are many times when it can be used with great effect.

Modern artists are to be congratulated for their having relegated cross-hatching, so popular twenty-five years ago, to the relatively unimportant place it deserves. At one time it was almost impossible to segregate the important lines of a drawing from the heavy patches of shading some popular artists had been pleased to inflict. The very word "shading" should tell us the manner in which it was meant to be used. At any rate, shading must always be secondary to the functional design even when it appears to be a part of that design.

The method of shading will differ with the medium employed in the drawing. And, quite naturally, if the drawing is to be reproduced, that too must be taken into consideration. For example, a pen and ink drawing will very likely be reproduced by means of a line engraving. However, if the artist has used his brush for shading, a halftone engraving will be called for. This will double the cost, and the fine line work will be impaired.

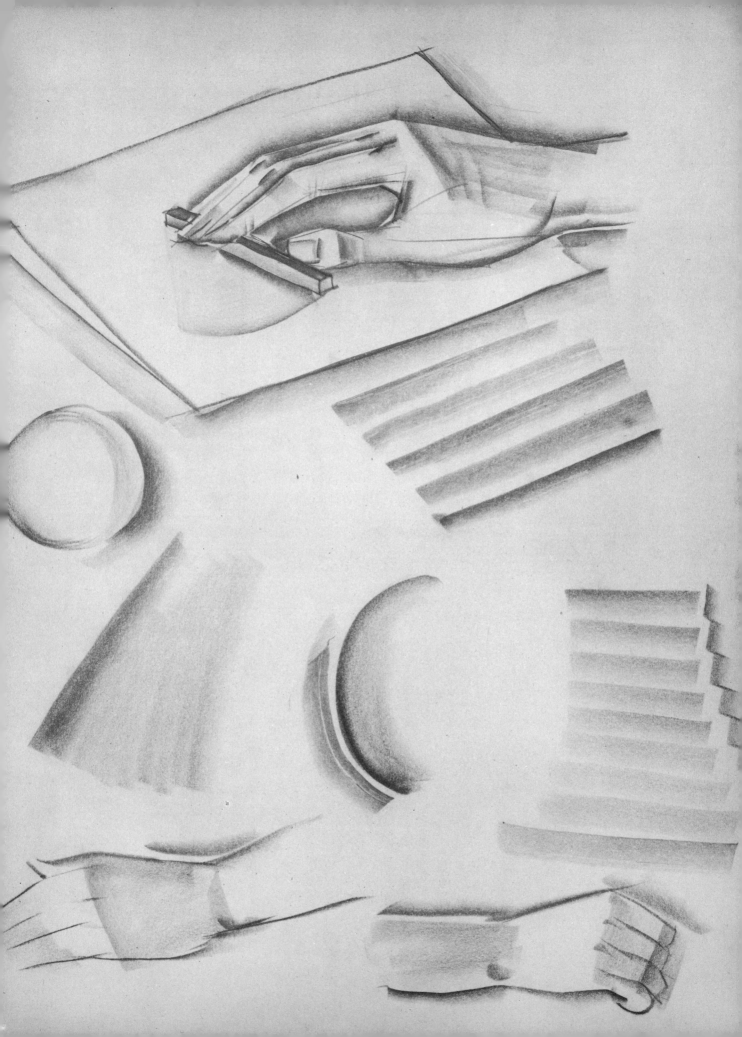

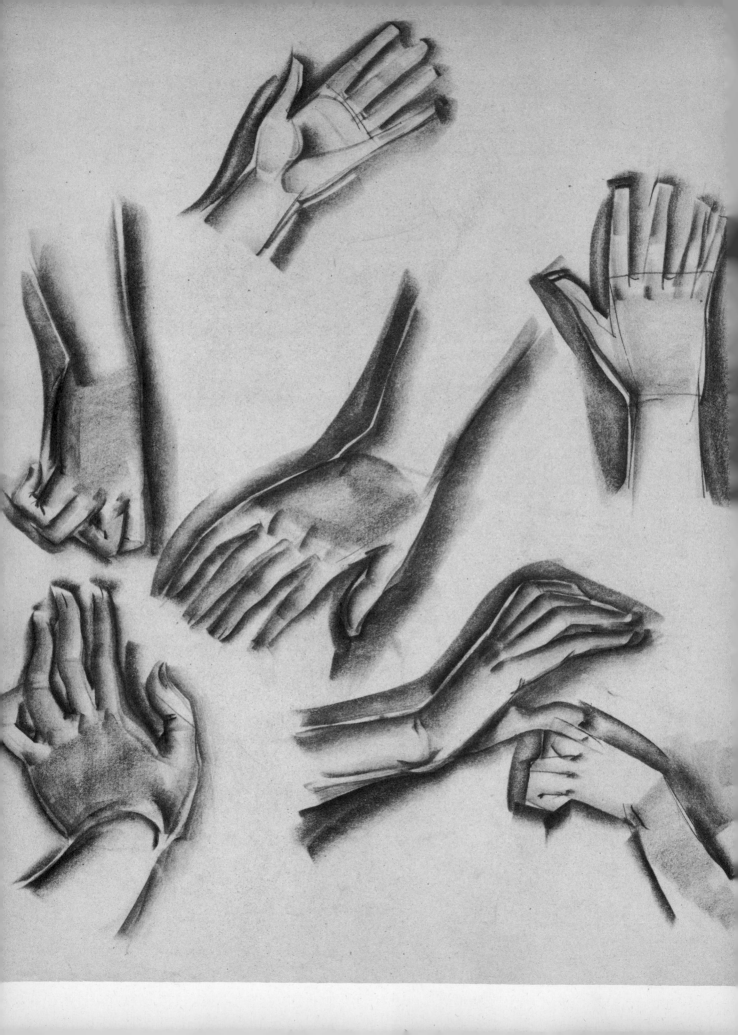

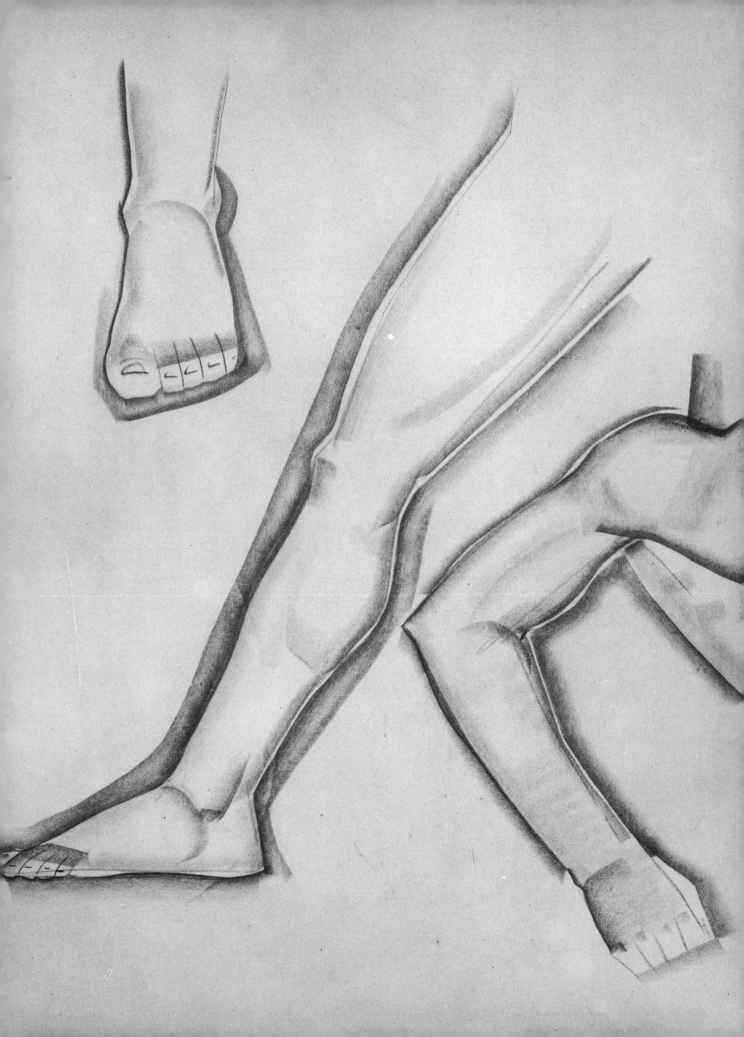

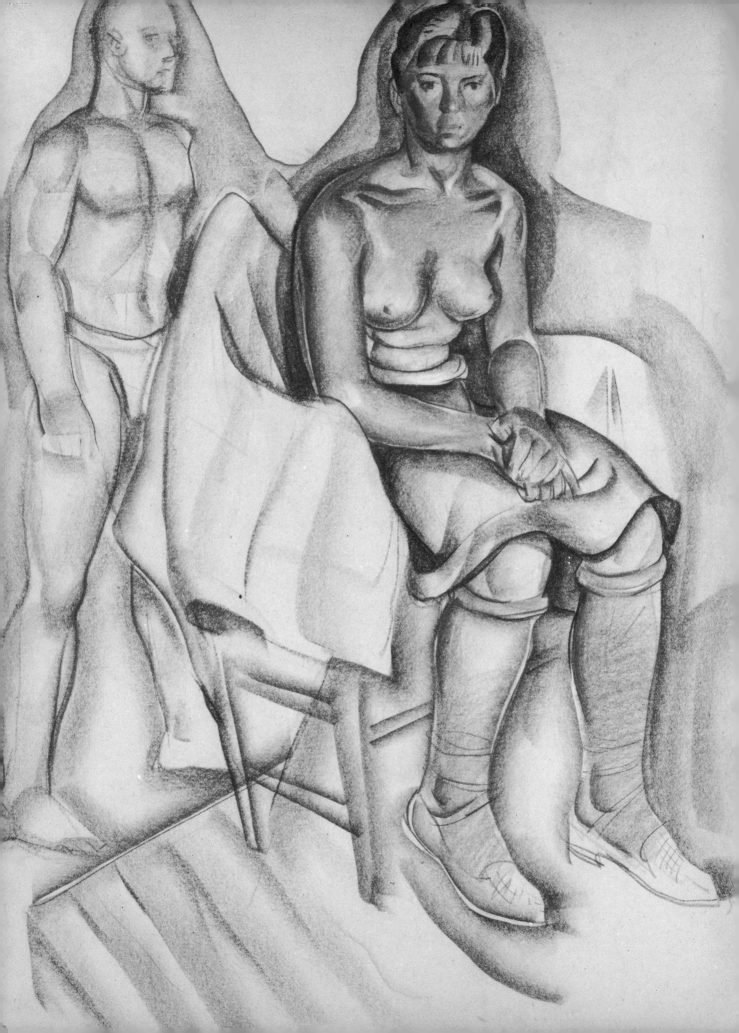

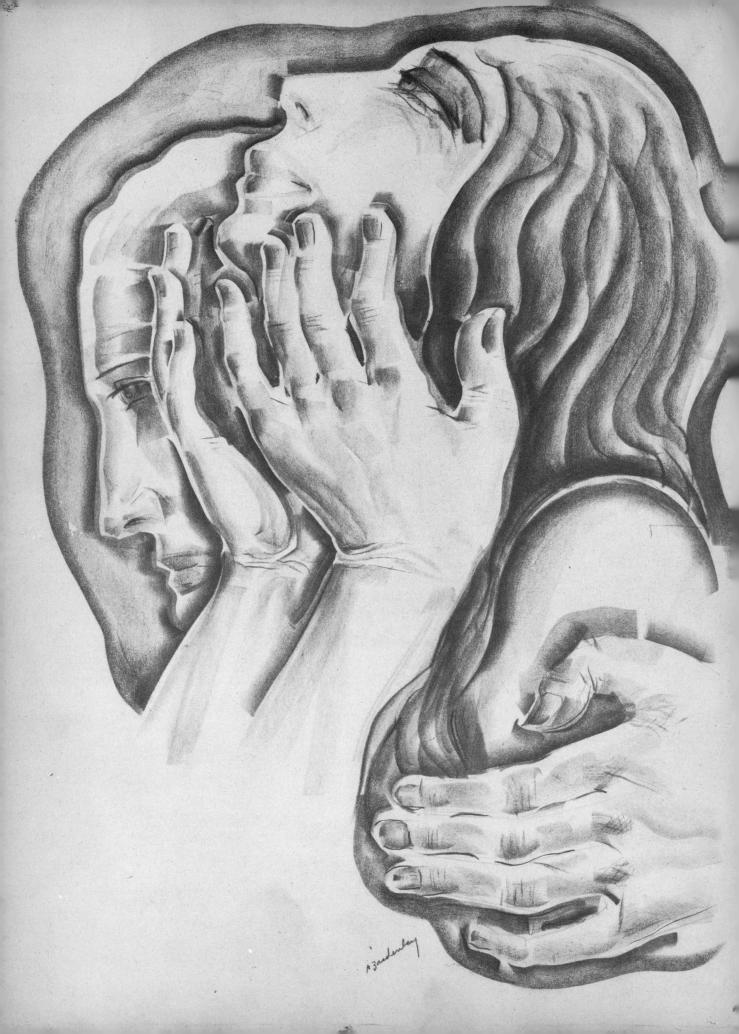

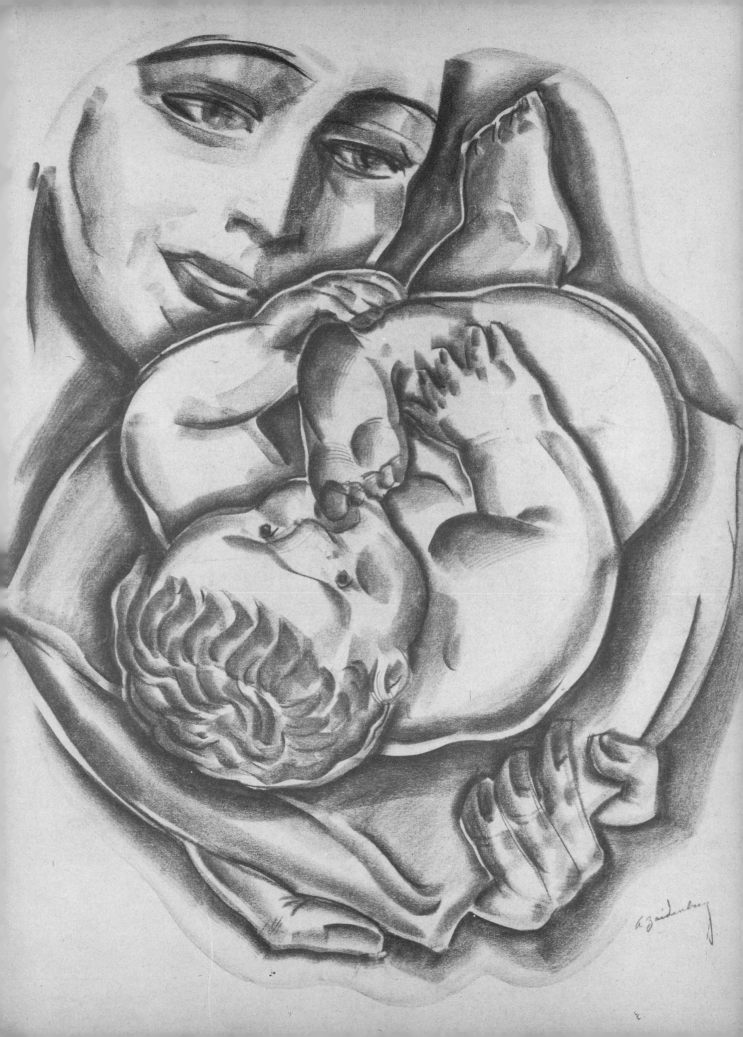

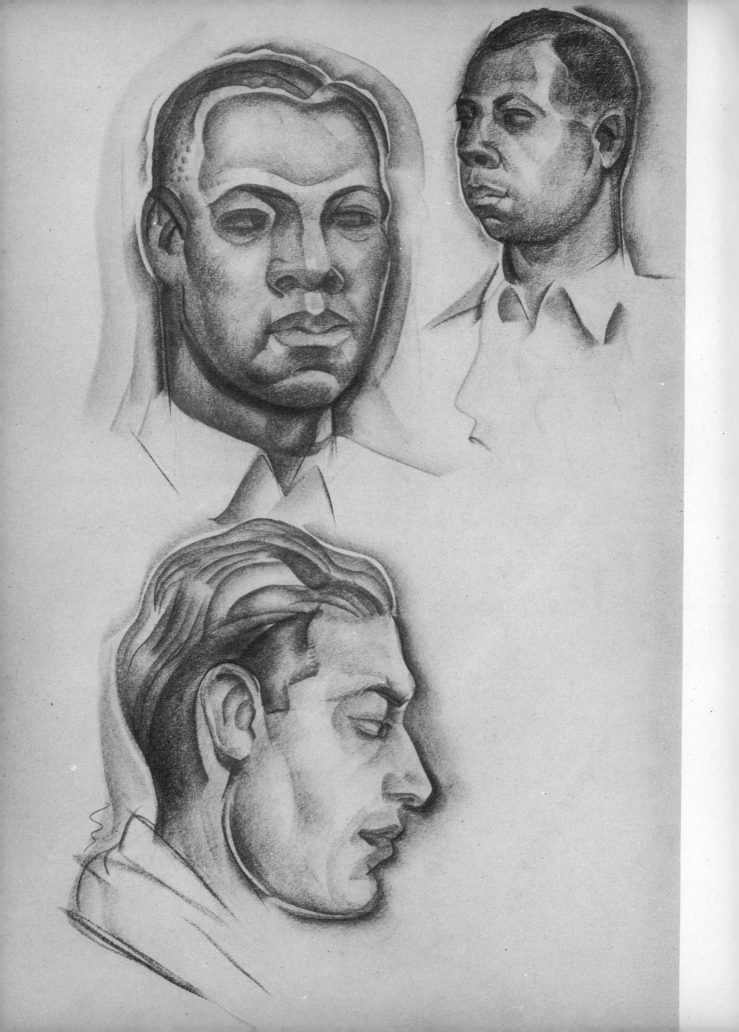

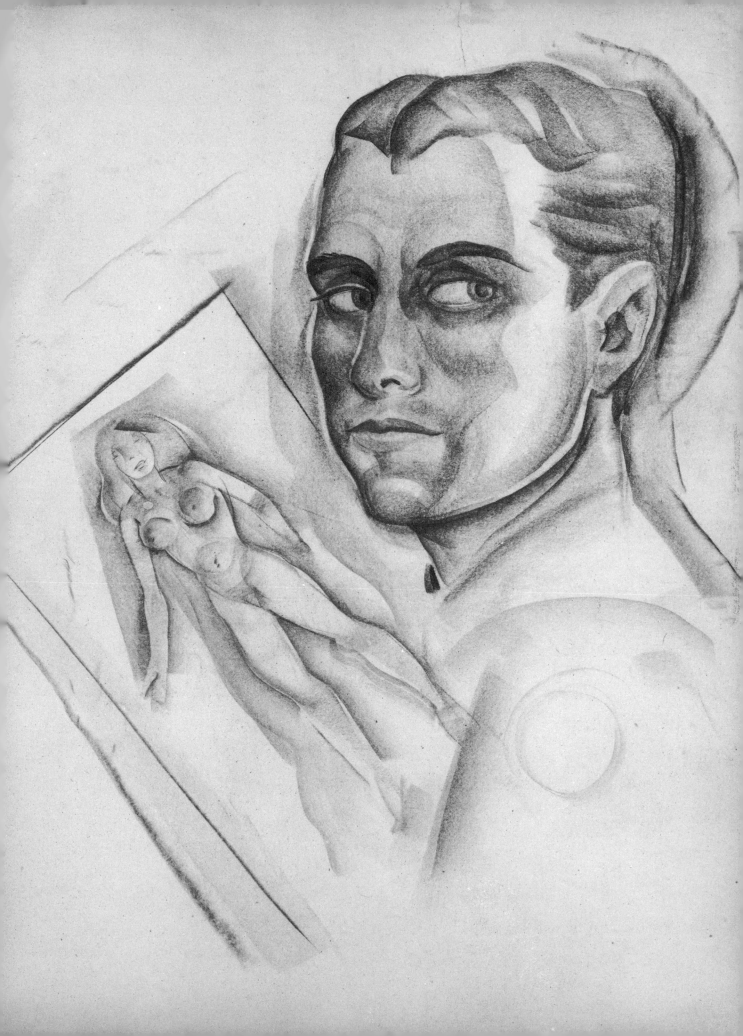

PART TWO
Animals

Once we have acquired a general knowledge of the anatomy of man, we have much less to learn about the general construction of backbone animals, for there is great similarity between the skeletons of the two classes of mammals.

Here again it should be urged that a thorough knowledge of anatomy is superfluous. However, for the purpose of showing the relationship between men and animals, the two plates which follow will outline their skeleton structures. You will notice that each has a backbone, pelvis, rib cage, skull, etc., etc.

Remember that when we were drawing humans we conventionalized the forms and arrived at their simple essence. And so, since we see that the underlying structure of animals is similar, we can use many of the same approaches.

There are two drawings of simple forms in the following plates. Using a circle for the rib area, another for the haunch area and the body slung between, gives a sound base for the approach in drawing any animal. The head can be reduced to a circle for each of the eye, brain and ear, and an oblong for the jaw, nose and muzzle area. The legs, though they vary in bulk and articulation in different animals, can be worked out in three forms, as with the leg of a man.

This should give you some idea about the drawing of animals in general. Later, we shall deal with specific animals.

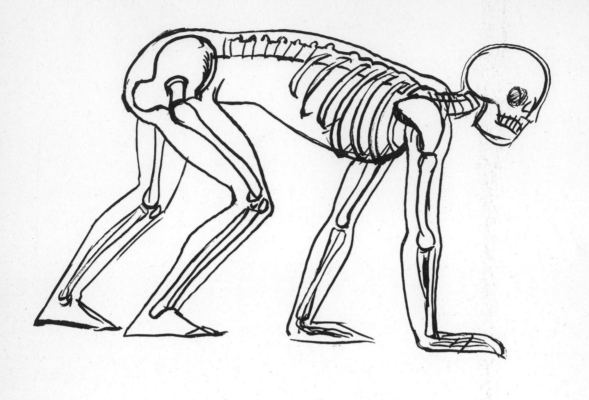
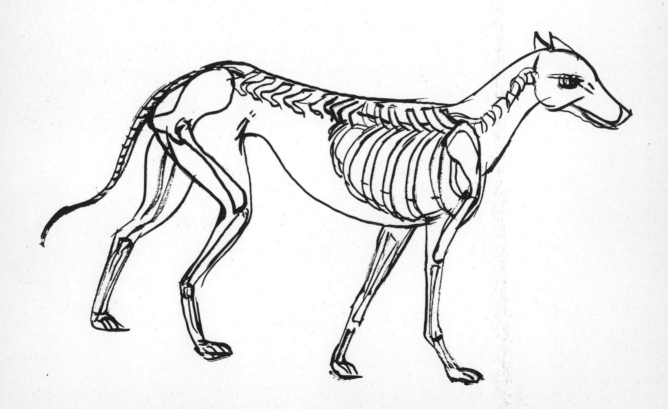

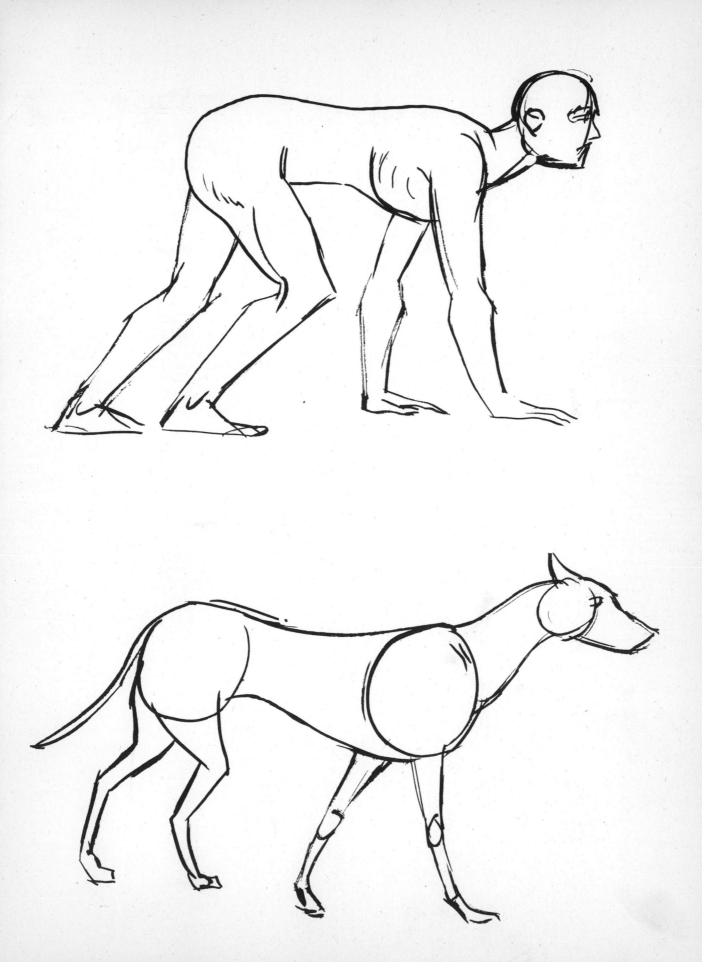

6 "

More important than the complete muscle study in the
drawing of alert and moving animals is the study of the salient muscles, the ones that convey the most strength and agility.
Your choice must be made with discrimination. Use long, flow-
ing tones which follow the movement, not short, abrupt ones
which stop it.

Muscle forms can be as much an element of design as spot-
ting color and surface characteristics. Shading should not ne-
gate the strength and design of your animal.

242

The Horse

Even professional artists of recognized ability become terrified at the prospect of drawing a horse—when they have the animal in front of them, as well as from memory.

Again, there are men who are outstanding at the drawing of horses. It is quite possible to spend years studying the various paces and gaits of the many different species of horses, their complicated skeletons and muscle structures. And, for certain purposes, it may be said that such study can prove both profitable and interesting.

Unless your time is unlimited, it would be well to limit your classification of horses into the several main types. The thoroughbred racehorse may be depicted by a general slenderizing and streamlining. His hocks are slimmer by far than those of the ordinary horse. The polo pony is usually several hands shorter in stature, as is the cow pony of the West. The latter is shaggier than the polo pony, and his head does not show the same tendencies of breeding. The work horse, sometimes typified by the percheron, is simulated by greatly exaggerating the limbs, hocks and muscle-centers.

Our primary interest, however, is rather different. We are concerned principally with learning how to draw horses in action, for the purpose of using them in those of our compositions which may require them.

243

TRUNK

In drawing the trunk of the horse it will be better that the student forgets, for the time being, the construction of the human figure. Although the limbs of an animal are in some ways similar to our arms and legs, the structure of the trunk is quite different.

This is due to the functions of the limbs approaching those of men, whereas in the trunk the peculiarities of each species takes on its own form. The outlines vary, the trunk of the horse being represented as an almost square mass. Muscles are bunched in different places and are used for different purposes.

It is advisable that you practice making small scale drawings. Draw two one-inch circles, and place them about three-quarters of an inch apart. Connect the circles at the top and bottom. (The lower connecting line joins the rear circle at a slightly higher point, as we have shown in the first plate following.)

These connected circles represent the entire mass of the body of the horse. The lines of the neck are almost parallel. Draw them so that they join the forward circle at the top and about midway down the front. Naturally, this horse will be facing right, in profile.

244

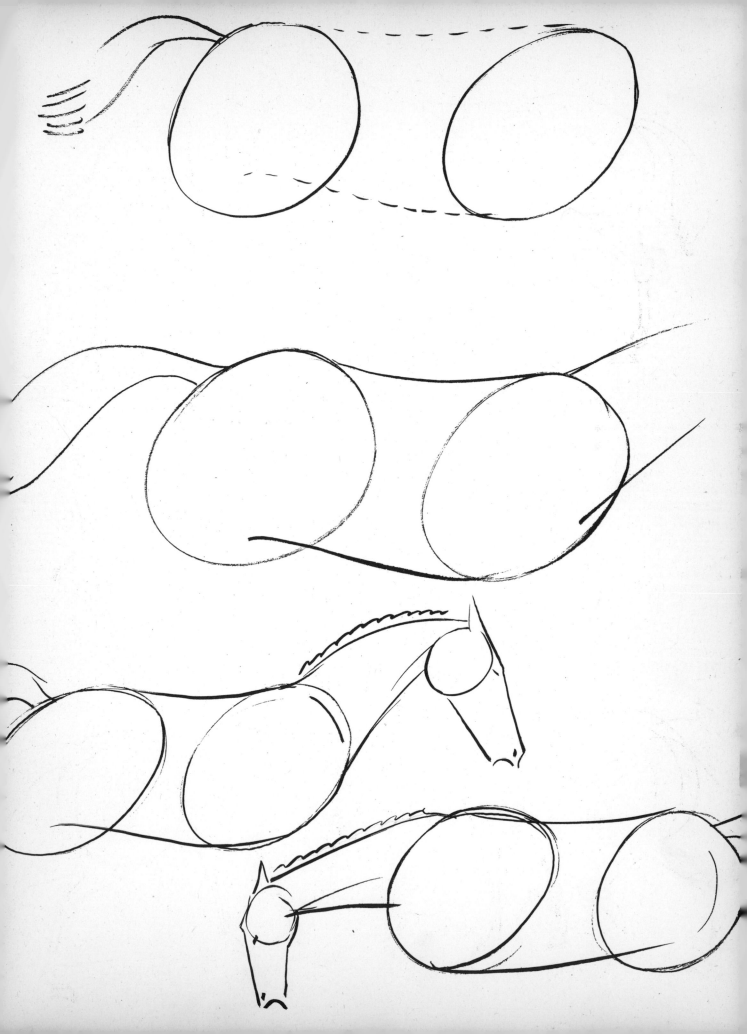

LEGS

The legs of the horse are generally regarded as being quite difficult to draw. However, if you divide them into their simplest forms you will have no trouble. In this chapter you will find the leg brought down to five forms. Study and practice the foreleg first.

1. The upper leg above the knee is an oblong joined to the circle at the top and tapering to the knee.

2. The knee can be reduced to a small circular form. It does not protrude far beyond the width of the upper oblong where they are joined together.

3. The lower leg is formed by two slender parallels which connect the circle of the knee and a similar small circle at the ankle bone.

4. Two short parallel lines inclined forward join the hoof to the ankle bone.

5. The hoof is a triangular form.

These forms hold true for the hind leg as well, but, as you may notice in the plate, there is a difference in articulation. A heavier upper leg joins the circular buttock form. It tapers sharply as it descends to the knee; it also inclines rearward from the upper joining place. (See the plate.) Although the foreleg resembles the human leg in that it bends back at the knee, the hind leg of the horse can bend forward only.

These simple axioms of leg behavior and construction will suffice to cover most difficulties found in giving the horse a graceful action.

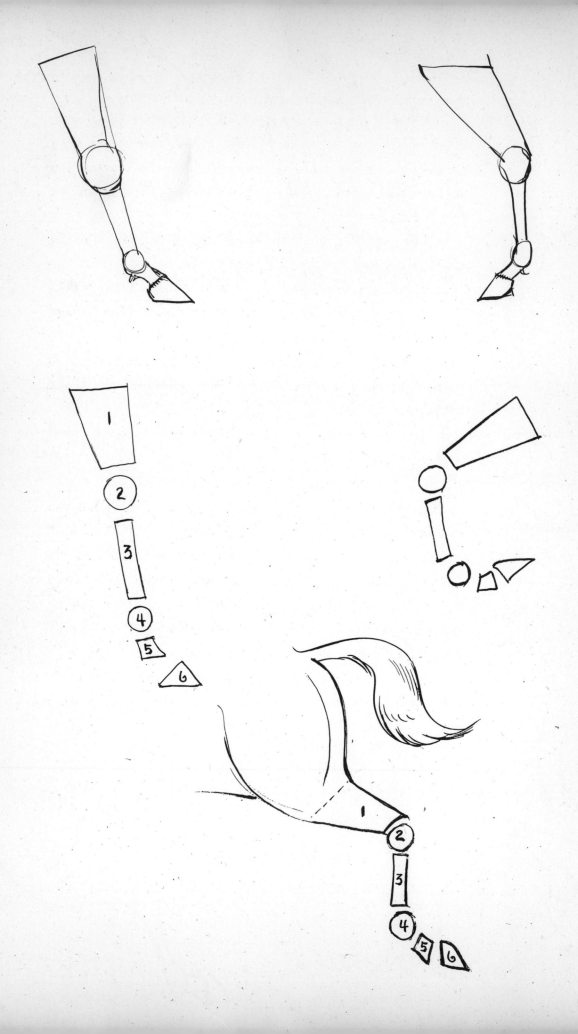

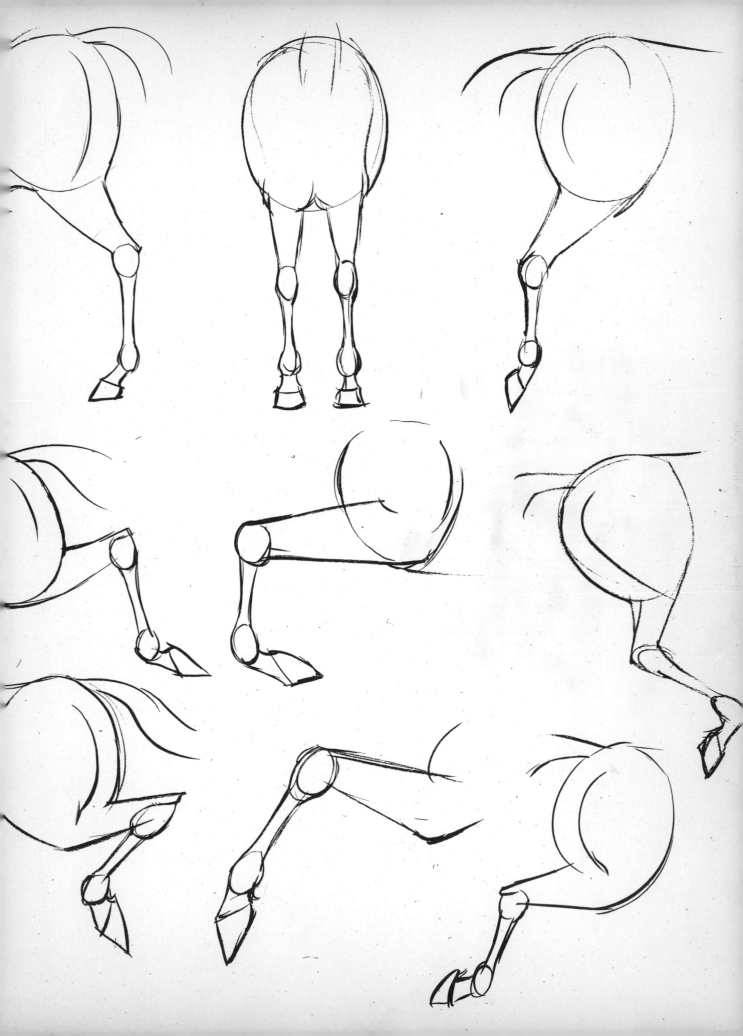

HORSE IN PERSPECTIVE

Now that you have analyzed the horse in his large simple forms, try turning him in various directions and actions: walking, running, jumping, etc.

When you turn the body of the horse, follow the same principles of foreshortening that you would use in drawing a glass from different positions.

As you turn the horse to a three-quarter view, the circles of the body overlap slightly and the connecting lines become foreshortened as is exemplified in the next plate. Follow this principle throughout your study of animal movement.

Do not make the mistakes that are so commonly found in the hunting and racing prints of the last century. You have very probably seen these prints, and so you will be familiar with the errors made by the artists. The most usual fault was depicting a horse jumping over a fence; the body of the horse was raised, but there was no show of action in his outline. The actual appearance is that of the horse being lifted from the ground by means of a pulley and invisible wires. A horse in motion is of course quite different. When drawing him make sure that the body is fore-shortened so that he will appear in his true perspective, a living thing.

The sketch by Vandyck, in the Gallery at the rear of this book, page 341, is an excellent example of the horse drawn in perspective.

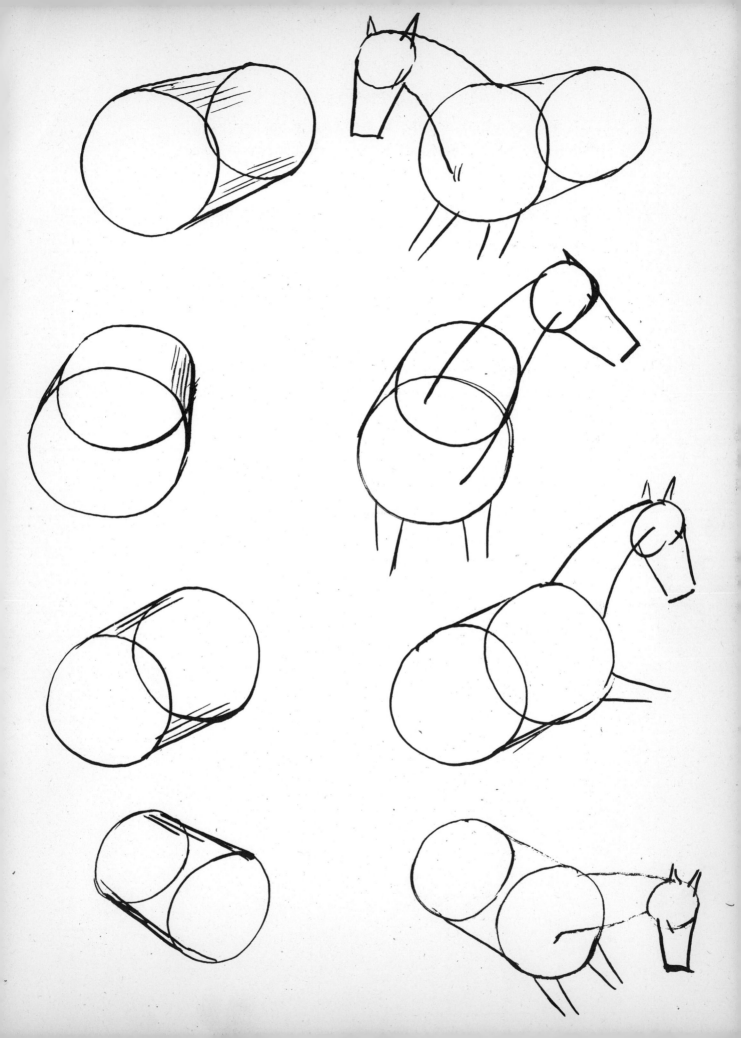

HEAD

Draw a small circle. To it attach the long and slightly tapering oblong which is the muzzle of the horse. Close to the front of the head, at the junction of the oblong and the circle, is the eye cavity.

Following the example indicated in the plates, practice turning these forms in different directions. Soon you will encounter no difficulty in drawing the outline of the head from any angle. Notice the point at which the circle joins the neck.

The head of the horse offers another opportunity to the student who desires to become proficient in animal portraiture. When we first took up the study of the horse we noted that the various types differed, to a greater or lesser degree, in their anatomical structure. The heads too are different, and in much the same way.

The head of the racehorse is sleek, the ears seem to lay back in a straighter line, and the nostrils flare more widely.

The saddle horse, which for Americans very often means a Morgan, is a sturdy specimen. His head is broader, the eyes are rounder and more intelligent.

The Western cow pony still shows traces of his Arabic descent. His features are smaller and slanted.

With the work horse, the artist is safe to coarsen most of his points, adding bulk and massiveness, dulling his features.

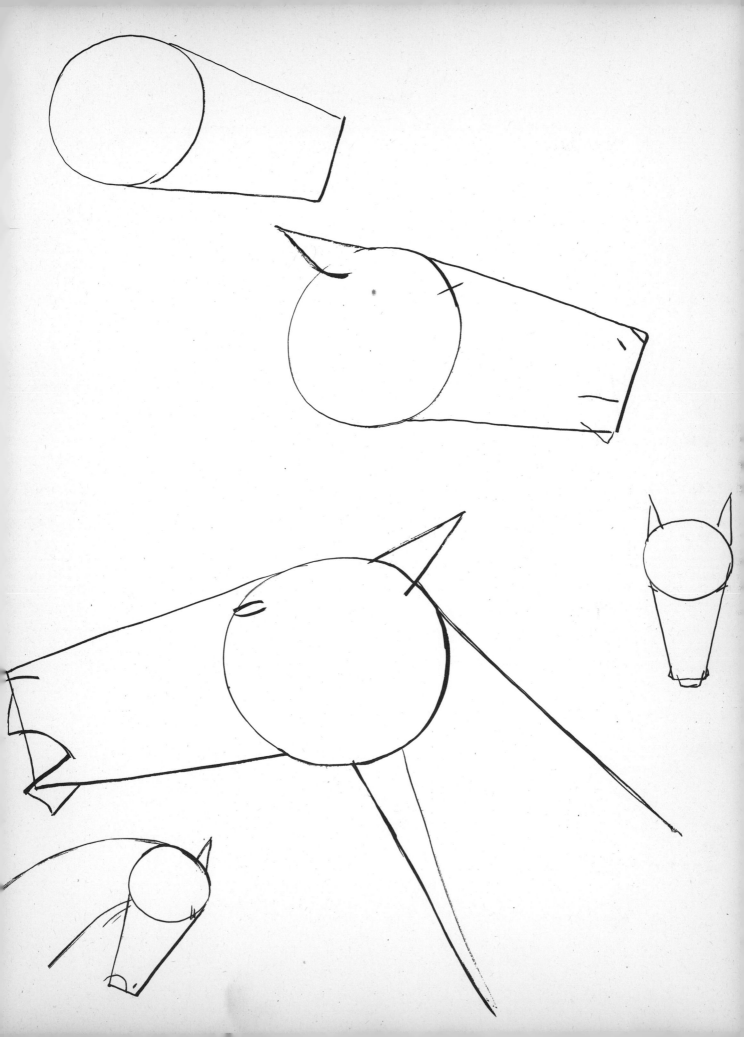

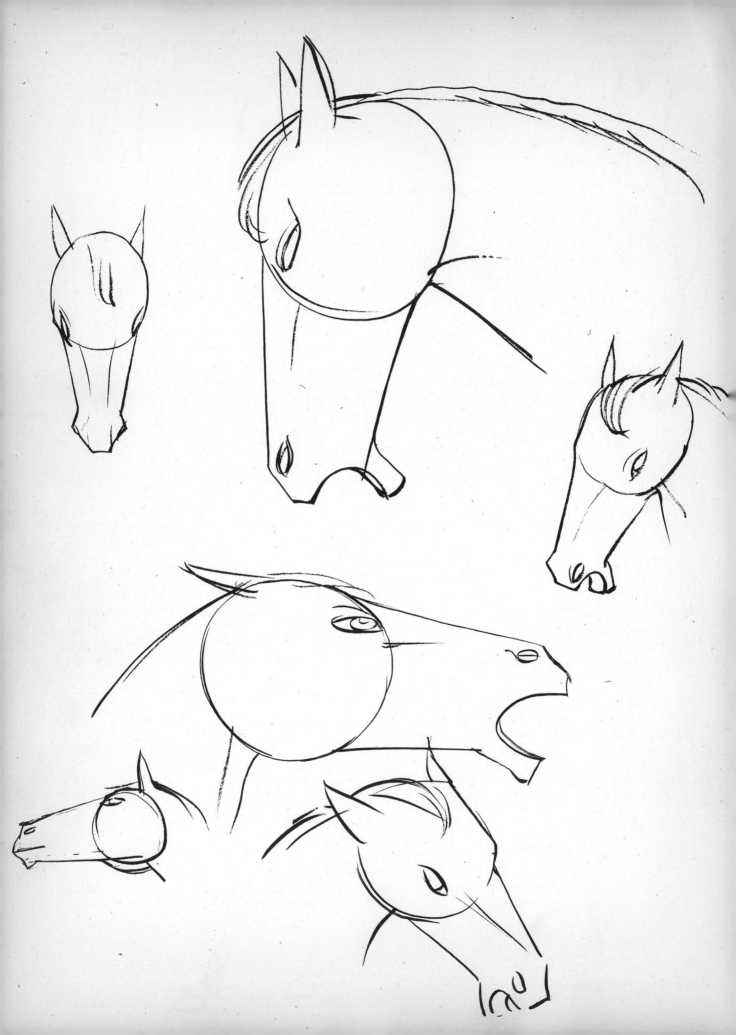

Paris 1937
A. Zaidenberg

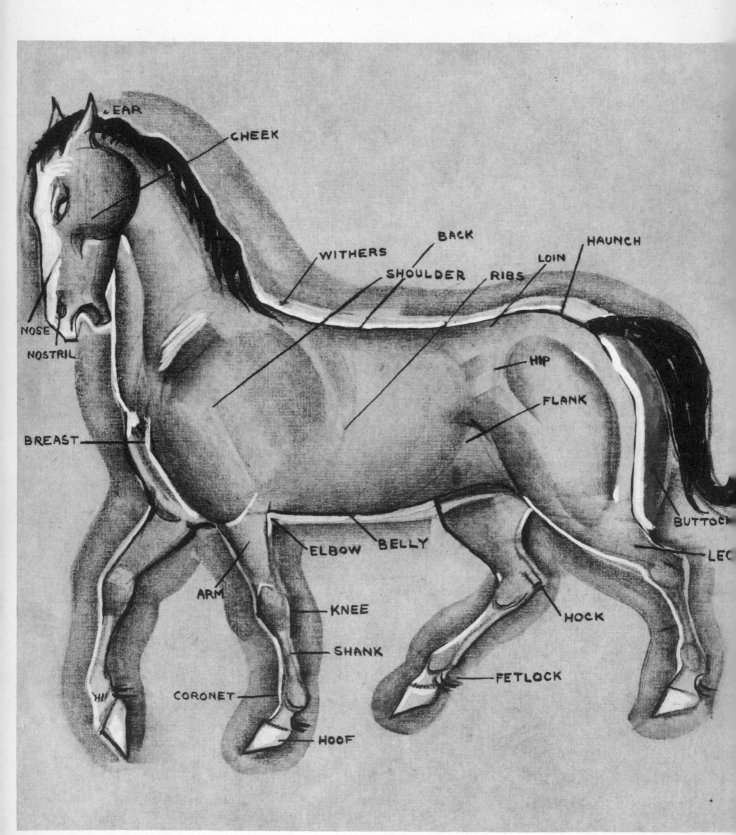

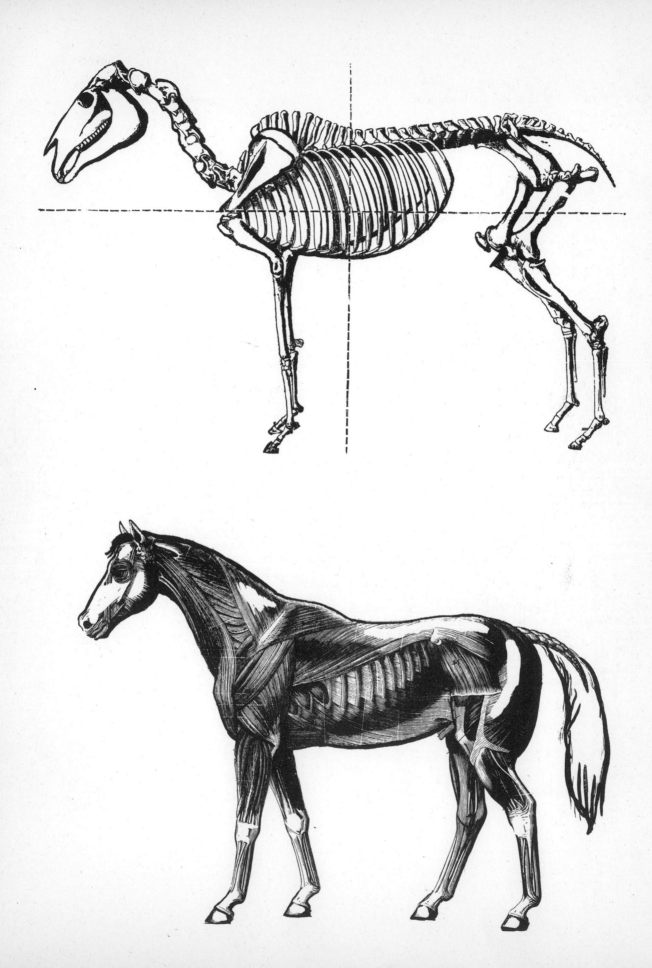

Other Animals

It is impossible to reduce the drawing of wild animals to a formula. The cat family is the one most often represented, perhaps because of the inherent grace and beauty of its members. But the more rarely depicted animals are not more difficult to draw; they require merely some slight study of their individual characteristics. For instance, the hyena most nearly approaches the dog in structure, but it possesses the peculiarity of having front and hind legs of different lengths. So it is with each animal: find its individual trait and accentuate it.

You will find that we shall approach these animals in much the same manner as we did the horse.

Two circles—one for the chest, one for the hindquarters—and the barrel of the body slung between them.

In the members of the cat family—lions, tigers, panthers, etc.—the neck is of course much shorter. But in character, general construction and action, they resemble the horse.

Follow these next few studies through their various stages and make a number of similar construction sketches. Using your imagination and powers of observation, proceed to make your animal drawings as individual as you please.

If you live in a large city utilize your local zoo. If none is available, your library will offer a number of excellent books from which you may take your models.

260

Tigers, Leopards and Panthers

Here are some studies of tigers, leopards and panthers.

The simplest way to differentiate between these three members of the cat family is of course by the design of their coats. However, there are other differences, perhaps slightly less obvious. The tiger is the greatest of the three. His markings are the most pronounced and his jaws are heaviest.

The leopard is spotted only for pictorial purposes. Actually his coat is quite like that of the panther. Only new-born leopard cubs possess spots, and they retain them for only a very short time after birth.

The panther is usually somewhat slighter than the leopard, but he is not possessed of quite so much grace in movement. His size, too, changes in accordance with his native habitat. The American panther, or mountain lion, appears to grow larger in the Rocky Mountains than in Florida.

From the preceding plates you have learned the approach toward getting action into the drawings of wild animals. Those that follow show them in various stages of repose; yet you will notice that there is always a sense of impending action. It is important to draw wild animals in a "fluid" manner. Swing your lines—there are no straight lines in cats.

Find and stress each significant form in the animal's pose.

264

STEALTH. A dry point

Elephants

Like Chinamen, most elephants seem the same to our untutored eyes. But, as any mahout could tell you, elephants are of two distinct types.

The elephant with which we are most familiar, through his appearances at zoos and with the circus, is the Indian elephant. He is somewhat smaller and a great deal more gentle. The Indian elephant has been trained to work.

The African elephant is of greater bulk and possesses a goodly amount of ferocity. He can rarely be trained to work and is sought mostly for his ivory. The tusks of the African elephant are longer and more curved than those of his Indian cousin.

Drawing the elephant offers almost the same problem as we found in drawing the horse. Use the method of circles, but in the case of the elephant it is wiser to use oval forms so that we may arrive at the animal's tall bulk. Support the great barrel of the body between the two ovals.

The leg articulation is somewhat different from that of the horse. The hind legs bend at the knee in the same manner as a human leg. Observe and practice the elephant's movements as indicated in the following plates.

Goats and Rabbits

These goats and rabbits were constructed along the same lines as were the other animals, but their characteristics of action and gait are very different. The rabbit, being a member of the rodent family, has of course a different backbone construction than that of the other animals we studied.

Again the two circles for the chest and the haunches, the barrel of the body being swung between them. The head of the goat is somewhat similar to that of the horse in its general construction.

Some very splendid and interesting studies have been made of goats and rabbits. We have seen an entire exhibition devoted to the subject.

Because of their beady eyes, tender noses, long ears and soft fur, rabbits make extremely interesting subjects for pictorial representation. The most famous rabbit of illustrative history was not a rabbit at all, in the true sense of the word. He was a hare, a larger and more sturdy member of the same family. We refer, of course, to Tenniel's drawing of the March Hare for Carroll's *Alice's Adventures in Wonderland*.

Monkeys

In drawing the monkey try to get the essence of his peculiar crouch, his long arms, the character of his gait.

If you can bring out the chief ape-like features, you will have accomplished all that can reasonably be expected of you, and your purpose will have been served.

To draw monkeys or any other animals in anatomical perfection would require the study of a life-time. There are, of course, countless species, and each of them differs in some way from the other.

We are concerned with learning to draw the "idea" of the monkey, rather than a photographic likeness of one particular type. Make frame studies like the one marked "A" in the plate. Try drawing them from other positions, bearing in mind that, except for gait and proportional differences, the framework will be similar to that of a man.

When it becomes apparent that you have succeeded in capturing the "monkeyish" manner of walk and stance on paper, superimpose the hairy pelt and other details.

Dogs

Again, except for differences in leg movement, the process is the same as in beginning the horse.

There are dogs of all sizes and breeds, but structurally they are very much the same. The differences lie mostly in muzzle, size, fur, ears and tail. Naturally, for these variations you must use your own powers of observation and memory.

The dog most popular in animal design today is the Scottish terrier. His oblong torso, short legs and blunt muzzle make him particularly adaptable for geometric repetition. His solidly black coat adds to the effectiveness. Other terriers approaching the Scotty in structure are the Sealyham, the Wire Hair, the Welsh, the Irish, and, of course, the Aberdeen.

Spaniels are quite different, their beautifully sad faces and silky hair possessing a great amount of charm. When drawing spaniels in action, it is advisable to ascertain whether the type you are using is actually suited for the work. There are a great number of different types of spaniels, and each of them is fitted by heritage and training for a particular job.

It is interesting to note that the little Pekingese, widely known as a lap dog, was the model used by Japanese and Chinese artists when they desired to depict the fierce and noble lion.

Following are a few common types of dogs; with each we have used the same method of approach.

277

Animals in Decorative Design

Here are a few plates showing etchings and woodcuts which use drawings of animals for decorative design.

You may notice that the previously outlined method of constructing animal forms lends itself to decorative treatment. The construction circles were purposely included in a number of places. This was done so that you may study the application of the principles you have learned.

Today, more than ever before, there is a growing demand for designs of animals. They appear in all manner of places: on women's clothes, on cravats, in cuff links and studs, and even on cracker boxes. In creating these designs it is important to remember that there must be more than just a representation of the animal; a geometric design is required in most cases, or at least a conventionalized pattern.

In order to use the animals appropiately, it is first necessary to reduce them to their simplest planes or forms. In that way they will be easier to handle, simpler to control and less likely to demand an over-complicated design.

PILGRIMAGE. A woodcut—areas to appear
white are cut away, leaving the lines of the
drawing that will print

EUROPA. A wood engraving

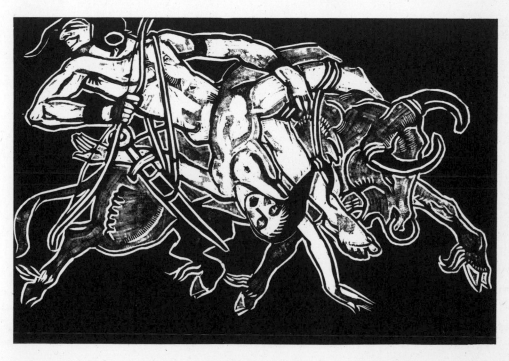

THE POOL. A woodcut, now on exhibition in
the Brooklyn Museum, New York

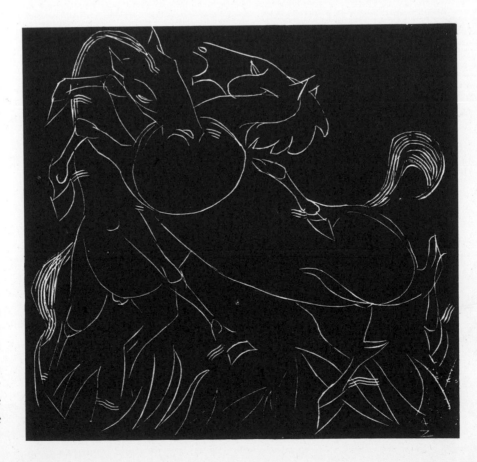

FIGHTING STAL-
LIONS. Intaglio lines in
this woodcut print white,
a principle directly opposite from the etched plate
wherein the engraved line
takes the ink

BULLFIGHT. An etching

Eight Animal Studies

Each of the following plates of animals have an analysis and a "finished" shaded study. In the shaded studies you may notice what appears to be complicated muscle structure. This is especially discernible in the two tiger and panther plates.

However, this is not muscle study in the photographic manner. The anatomy has been subordinated to the design, and the lines and points of stress have been exaggerated to achieve the expression of most power.

In the cat, the study of stealthy grace and latent power is the chief objective, and the circle method is to be used pliantly.

The mule is much the same as the horse, except for such surface differences as the eye, ear, tail, etc.

PART THREE

Composition

The figures and animals you have learned to draw may, of course, be used together as well as alone. And so now we shall group them, with an analysis of their basic structures.

It is essential to the composition of a picture that all the parts be so arranged as to form a homogeneous "story." Used here, "story" does not mean merely a literal tale, but also an impression or an emotional expression. Elements disturbing to the telling of your story should be avoided.

The ancient Greeks said, "The gods geometrize." And they followed the gods in achieving their greatest works of art, from building the Parthenon to their beautifully proportioned and designed sculpture of humans.

Artists have always sought the *"line juste"* and the "significant form."

There is no one coverall, no one formula for good composition, but it is safe to state that should your arrangement of figures arrive at such basic geometric forms as triangles or circles, should they follow along a diagonal or be symmetrically balanced, then you will have a well coordinated composition—a "picture."

294

TRIANGULAR

CIRCULAR

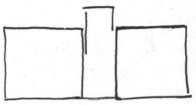

BI-SYMETRICAL

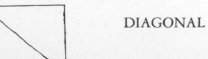

DIAGONAL

OVAL composition with triangular point of interest

OVAL

DIAGONAL

SEMICIRCLE

ZIGZAG MOTIF

PART FOUR
Design

The next composition will show the basic steps which are necessary to take in order to arrive at a somewhat intricate design.

The result is a combination of three of the geometric designs used in previous compositions. Included are the "W" design of the grouping on page 298, the triangle and the bisymmetrical balanced form. You will notice how the varied tonal values in shading give foreground, middle ground and background plans to the drawings.

Design is really only a continuation and variation of a simple form. Try creating one of your own. In a single column, or on a single line, draw a number of small circles or O's. Place them so that each just touches the one before it. Now draw a dot in the center of each circle. Then connect the widest parts of the circles with a series of little arcs. Your result will be a border design, simple yet effective. Now try the same thing with little squares. Add ornaments of your own conception. It will readily be seen that a great deal of ingenuity is not required for the creation of an interesting design, merely a clear eye and a logical mind.

The halftone compositions which follow are really quite simple in arrangement. Study them to discover the geometric designs on which they were based.

Although some critics are fond of stating that the great masters of the past managed to do well enough without resorting to any elaborate plan or design, this opinion is highly problematical. It is true that no great work was accompanied by an explanatory note which showed how the artist arrived at his conclusion, but the same holds true today with artists who state in unequivocal terms their dependency on and belief in the planned design as a forerunner of any composition.

William Blake, whose genius went unrecognized until very recently, often neglected the more conventional aspects of representation in order to adhere to a very definite and fixed design. By doing this he achieved a unity of purpose and composition that was integral in its fulfillment. And it is because of this single quality that in some respects the work of Blake has rarely been equalled, almost never surpassed.

On page 320 of this book we shall see that the great Albrecht Dürer even went so far as to teach the drawing of the human figure according to mathematical principles. And so it is easy to understand that if a single figure is based upon a precise formula, then certainly it is equally important to accord the entire painting or drawing at least the modicum of a plan.

Artists who try to execute their compositions without first conceiving a design, are either doomed to failure or else they have chosen a subject which has a design within itself.

It is strange to note that we must travel back to the time when men first began to draw in order to find work which was design pure and simple. According to the writings of Plato, that period is placed at approximately 10,000 years before the Birth of Christ. At that time men drew only in outline, and so design

300

was an elementary and obvious thing. But as civilization and the arts progressed, pictured representation grew more complicated, and the lesser artists (who were, of course, in the great majority) became so involved with detail that they lost the functional purpose of all graphic art: DESIGN.

Perhaps the worst phase of artistic endeavor was coincidental with the Roman mastery of the known world. Through the centuries of Roman rule, only seven or eight artists attained any distinction at all, and these were decidedly inferior to the best. Yet at the same time, in the Americas and elsewhere, other civilizations were producing beautifully designed works of art—achievements which have stood the tests of time and comparison.

We sometimes speak of the Dark Ages as though of a period barren of artistic endeavor. This is not exactly true, because there were any number of men who continued to sketch and paint and draw. However, they did fail to attain any notable success, for the very good reason that their work was cluttered and fussy, and—most important—they had lost sight of the principles of design.

Then came the Renaissance, and once again the artists looked upon their work as something more than a representation of static figures. They grew serious, and while studying to learn their own deficiencies, discovered that fundamental design must be applied to every composition, simple or elaborate.

And so we see that from Botticelli, da Vinci and Dürer, through Rubens, Blake and Renoir, to Picasso and Salvador Dali, every artist worthy of the name adhered to the principles of design and planned his compositions accordingly.

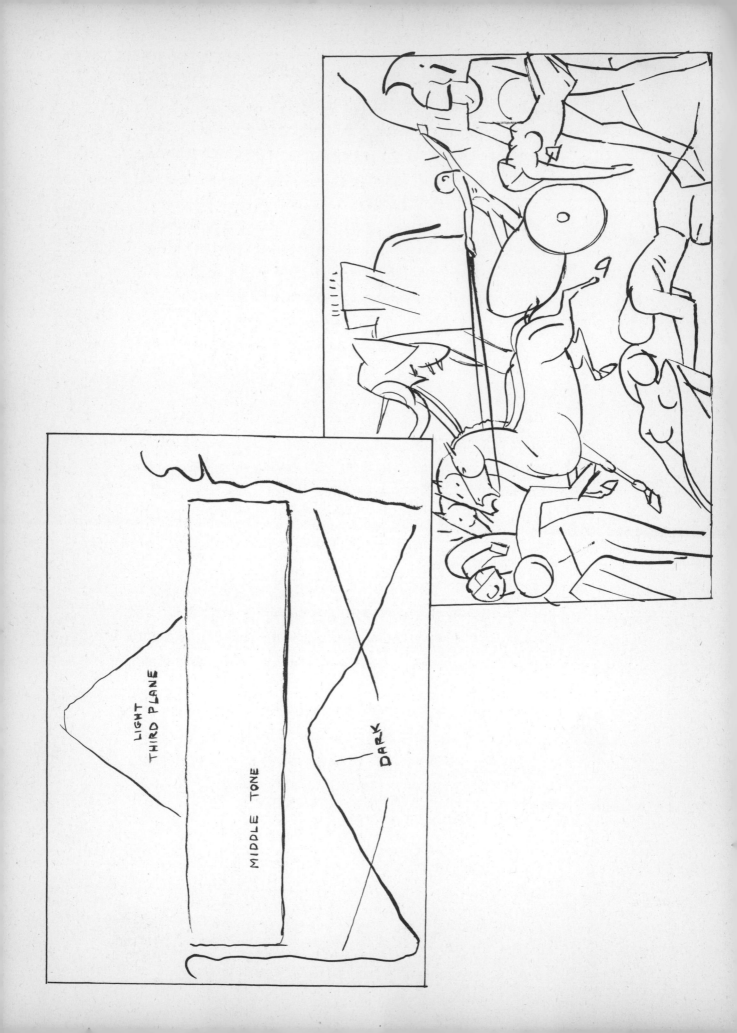

A charcoal drawing for Flaubert's *Salammbo*

Another illustration for *Salammbo*

A charcoal drawing for Renan's *Life of Jesus*

Another illustration for *Life of Jesus*

THE RED CUP. One of a series of four oil paintings in a recent Surrealist Exhibition, Paris.

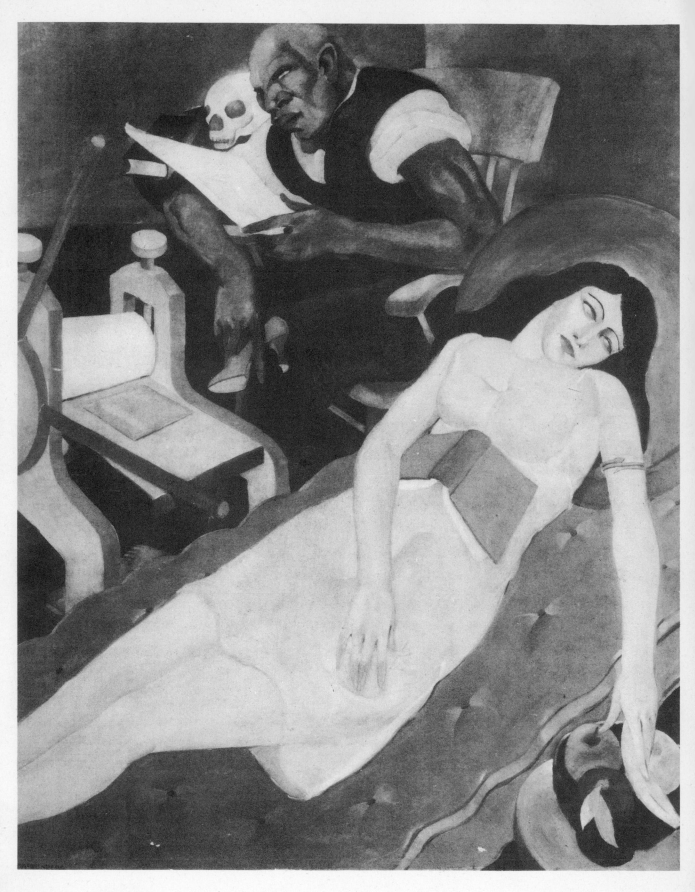

MILTON'S STUDIO

PART FIVE

Gallery OF DRAWINGS BY THE WORLD'S GREAT MASTERS

The remaining pages bring you a selection of drawings from the hands of great artists. They will illustrate that the simple approach and the elimination of non-essential details have created some of the world's great works of art.

Quite naturally, volumes could be and have been written about the works included herein, and still more volumes about the artists themselves. But despite this eminent, if implausible, possibility, enough material has been gathered to serve our full purpose. Among these reproductions may be found several to which especial reference was made in the main body of the foregoing text. The grouping has been done chronologically, so that there will be no misunderstanding as to our preferences and prejudices. Wherever possible we shall point out such features which the student should be able to link with the lessons that have gone before.

The eyes in the portrait of a young man, by Botticelli, are of particular interest. Note the beautiful drawing which went into the few forms used to depict those passionate depths.

The artist was a Florentine painter and engraver who was born in 1437 and died in 1515. He studied under Filippo Lippi, and subsequently visited Rome, where he executed several important works for Pope Sixtus IV. His chief works at Florence were a *Venus Attired by the Graces,* and a *Venus Anadyomene;*

309

Botticelli's Portrait of a Young Man

also an *Assumption of the Virgin,* in Saint Peter Maggiore, highly praised by Vasari, and now in England. It contains a multitude of figures in the heavens, the Apostles around the Tomb from which the Virgin has ascended and the kneeling figures of Palmieri and his wife. Palmieri had commissioned Botticelli to do the painting. Baldini's engravings for Dante's *Inferno* were modeled from the designs of this master.

The self portrait by Leonardo da Vinci is a masterpiece of honest drawing. Drawn in a few lines and with a minimum of shading, it stands as an unexcelled piece of fine portraiture.

This illustrious artist, called by Lanzi *The Father of Modern Painting,* was also an eminent sculptor, architect and engineer, the natural son of Pietro da Vinci, notary to the Florentine Republic. He was born in Lower Valdarno, at the castle of Vinci, in 1452. At an early age he evinced remarkably quick abilities for everything he turned his attention to, but more particularly for arithmetic, music and drawing. His drawings seemed wonderful to his father, who showed them to Andrea Verocchio, and that celebrated artist, greatly surprised at seeing productions of such merit from an uninstructed hand, willingly took Leonardo as a pupil. He was soon much more astonished when he perceived the progress his pupil made; he felt his own inferiority, and when Leonardo painted an angel in a picture of the *Baptism of Christ* so much superior to the other figures that it rendered the inferiority of Verocchio apparent to everyone, he relinquished the pencil forever.

The talents of Leonardo soon attracted public attention at Florence. He was endowed by nature with a genius uncom-

311

Self-portrait by Leonardo da Vinci

monly elevated and penetrating, eager after discovery, and diligent in pursuit, not only in what related to sculpture and architecture, but also in the accomplishments of horsemanship, fencing and dancing. Unlike most men of versatile talent, he was so perfect in all these, that when he performed any one, observers were ready to imagine that it must have been his sole study.

To such vigor of intellect he joined an elegance of features and of manners that graced the virtues of his mind. He was affable with strangers, with citizens, with private individuals and with princes. This extraordinary combination of qualities in a single man soon spread his fame over all Italy.

Leonardo's life may be divided into four periods, the first of which includes the time he remained in Florence, until 1494. Throughout his entire life he retained traces of his early education. Like Verocchio, he designed more readily than he painted; he assiduously cultivated mathematics; in his design and in his countenances he prized vivacity of expression more than dignity and fullness of contour; he was very careful in drawing his horses and in representing the skirmishes of soldiers; and he was more solicitous about improving his art than about multiplying his pictures. By his knowledge of sculpture he gave that perfect relief and roundness, in which painting was then wanting; he imparted to it symmetry, grace and spirit, and these and his other merits gave him the title of the Father of Modern Painting.

He had two styles, the one abounding in shadow, which gives brilliance to the contrasting lights; the other more quiet and managed by middle tints. In each style, the grace of his design, the expression of the affections, and the delicacy of his pencil, are unrivalled. Everything is lively: the foreground, the landscape, the adventitious ornaments of necklaces, flowers and architecture; but this gaiety is more apparent in the heads. In this he seemingly repeats the same idea, and gives them a smile which delights the mind of a spectator.

The second period of Leonardo's life begins with his residence in Milan. About 1490 he presented a memorial to the Duke Lodovicio Sforza, in which he set forth at considerable length his abilities in painting, sculpture, architecture and engineering. Accordingly, in 1494, the Duke invited him to Milan and appointed him Director of the Academy of Painting and Architecture, which he had recently revived with additional splendor and encouragement. During his residence there, da Vinci's painting activity was mostly confined to his celebrated *Last Supper*. As director of the Academy, he abolished all the dry, Gothic principles of his predecessor, Michelino, and introduced the beautiful simplicity and purity of the Roman and Grecian style.

The Duke engaged Leonardo in the stupendous project of conducting the waters of the Adda, from Mortesana, through the Valteline and the Valley of the Chiavenna, to the walls of Milan, a distance of nearly two hundred miles. Sensible to the greatness of this undertaking, Leonardo applied himself more closely to those branches of philosophy and mathematics which are most adapted to mechanics, and he finally accomplished this immense work, greatly to the astonishment and admiration of all Italy. In 1500 the Duke was overthrown in battle by the French, made prisoner and conducted to France,

314

where he soon died. The Academy was suppressed, the professors dispersed, and Leonardo, after losing all, was obliged to quit the city and take refuge in Florence.

The third period began in 1502 when Cesare Borgia, captain-general in the Pope's army, appointed Leonardo his chief architect and engineer, and the artist visited many parts of Rome in his official capacity. The Pope died the next year and Leonardo returned to Florence. There he was employed by Soderini to paint one side of the Council Hall of the Palazzo Vecchio, while Michelangelo, then in his twenty-ninth year and already rising to eminence, was fixed upon as the artist to paint the other side.

The fame of this contest between the two great artists caused much excitement and induced Raphael, who had recently quit the school of Perugino, to visit Florence. The grace and delicacy of Leonardo's style, compared with the dry Gothic manner of Perugino, excited the admiration of the young Raphael, and inspired him with a more modern taste.

Leonardo's final departure from Rome marked his relinquishment of the art of painting and the start of the fourth period of his life. He set out for Pavia at the invitation of Francis I. of France, who received him with the greatest kindness and took him into his service, with an annual salary of 700 crowns.

Leonardo accompanied the King to Bologna, where he went to meet Leo X., and afterwards, in the beginning of 1516, he accompanied him to Florence. The health of this great painter was so much enfeebled after leaving Italy, that he executed little more. The King could not prevail upon him even to color his cartoon of St. Anna, which he had brought with him; nor

315

did he seem disposed to commence any new work which would require the exertion of his energies. During an indisposition of five years he continued to receive marks of the King's esteem. His health gradually grew worse, and he finally expired at Fontainebleau on May 2nd, 1519, at the age of sixty-seven. His greatness has never since been surpassed, and his Treatise is still studied by painters of today.

Less than twenty years after the birth of Leonardo, in 1471, Albrecht Dürer was born at Nuremberg. However, despite his birthplace, Dürer was in reality a Hungarian, his father having settled in the more northerly city only a few years before the artist was born. The father was a skillful goldsmith, and it was he who taught Dürer his first rudiments of design, intending him for his own profession. Young Dürer showed such inclination for the arts and sciences, however, that his father permitted him to follow the bent of his genius.

Though Dürer was most famous as an engraver, yet he executed many large paintings which occupy a distinguished place in the collections of Germany and other European countries. At Munich are some of the most famous, such as *Adam and Eve,* the *Adoration of the Magi,* the *Crucifixion,* the *Crowning of the Virgin,* the *Battle between Alexander and Darius,* and many other great works.

But it was as an engraver that Dürer derived most of his fame, and he is allowed to have surpassed every artist of his time in this branch of the art—nor has it been surpassed to this day. When we consider that, without any models worthy of imitation, he brought engraving to such great perfection,

316

Imperator Cæsar Diuus Maximilianus Pius Felix Augustus

KAISER MAXIMILIAN I by Dürer. Metropolitan Museum of Art

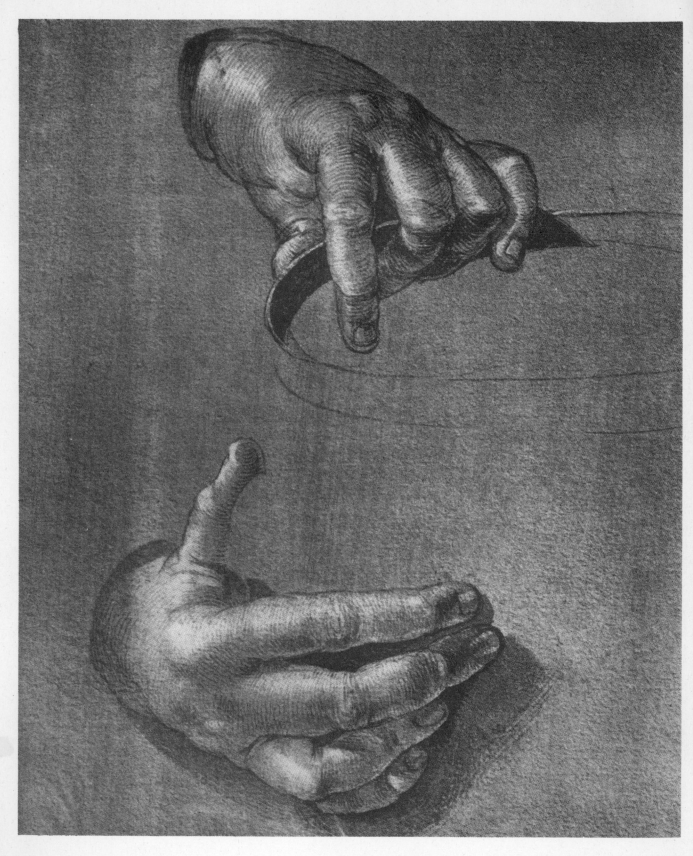

Dürer's hands, self-drawn

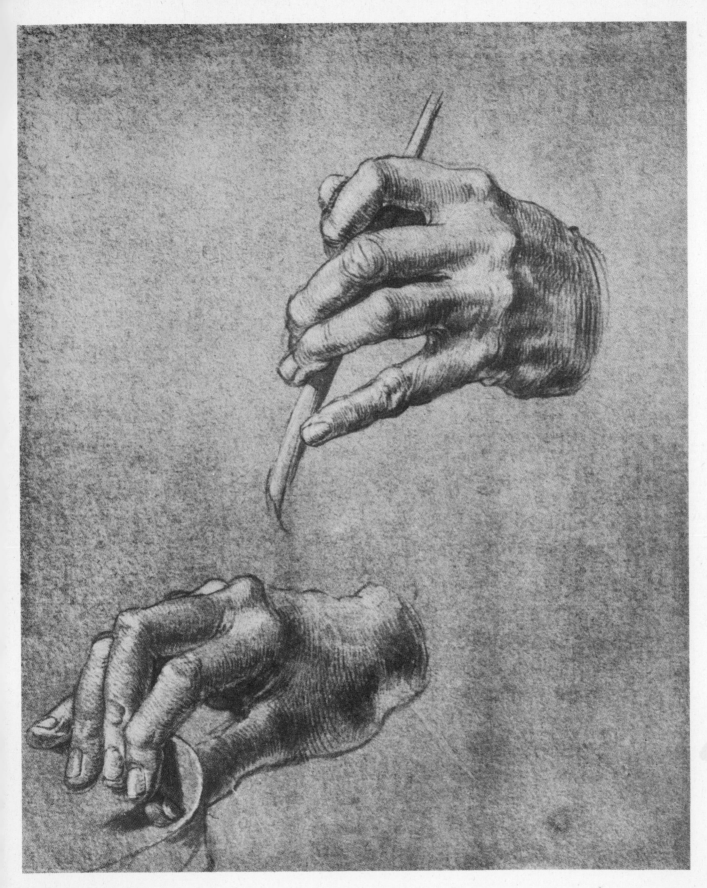

Dürer's hands, self-drawn

we are astonished at his genius and at his own resources. Although engraving has had the advantage and experience of more than four centuries, it would perhaps be difficult to select a specimen of excellence in execution surpassing his print of St. Jerome, engraved in 1514. He had a perfect command of the graver, and his works are executed with remarkable clearness and neatness of stroke; if we do not find in his plates that boldness and freedom desirable in large historical works, we find in them everything that can be wished in works more minute and more finished.

The Emperor, Maximilian I., had a great esteem for him and appointed him court painter with a liberal pension, and conferred on him letters of nobility. Ferdinand, King of Hungary, also bestowed upon him marked favors and liberality. Dürer was in favor with high and low. All the artists and learned men of his time honored and loved him, and his early death in 1528 was universally lamented. He always lived in a frugal manner, without the least ostentation for the distinguished favors heaped upon him. He applied himself to his profession with the most constant and untiring industry, which, together with his great knowledge, great facility of mechanical execution, and a remarkable talent for imitation, enabled him to rise to such distinction and to exert so powerful an influence on the character of German art for a great length of time. He was the first artist in Germany who practiced and taught the rules of perspective, and of the proportions of the human figure, according to mathematical principles.

Dürer often contorted shapes to exaggerate the character he was drawing; some of the hands shown in this gallery are ex-

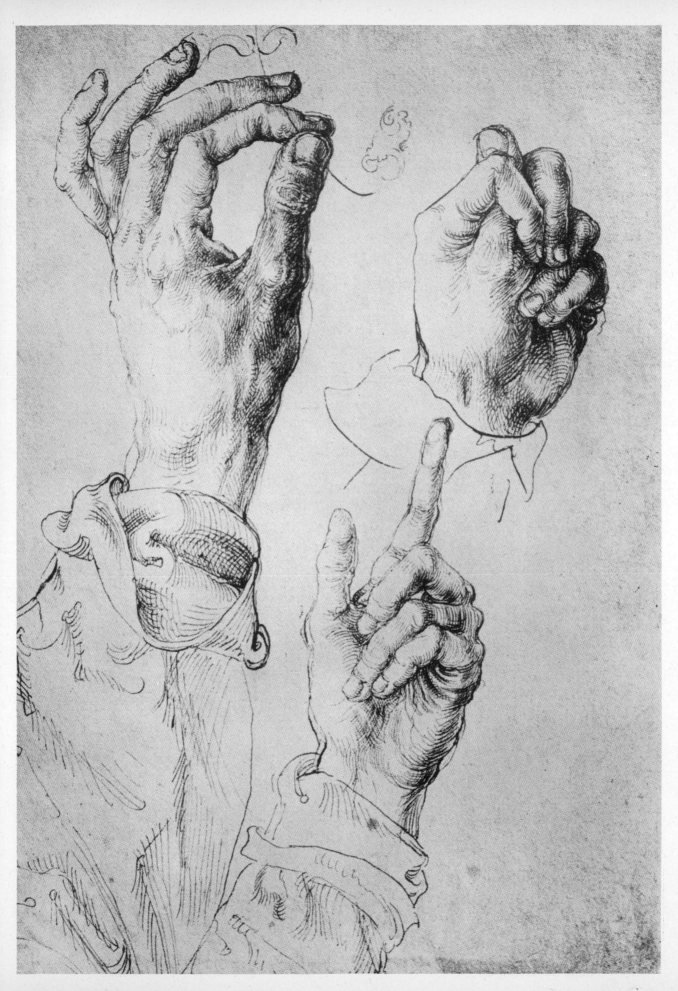

Studies of Dürer's left hand

amples of that tendency. However, the contortions are built on top of solid construction, and his division of the fingers and backs of hands into planes and solid forms can be discerned in the shading.

Represented here by his Sketch for the *Head of a Sybil,* is the artist who painted the other side of the Council Hall of the Palazzo Vecchio. Michelangelo (Buonarotti) was born in 1474 at the castle of Caprese, in Tuscany, of which fortress his father was the governor. He was descended from the noble family of Canosa, which he rendered still more illustrious by the productions of his mighty genius. His father intended him for one of the learned professions, and placed him in a grammar school at Florence. Here the young Angelo soon manifested great fondness for drawing, and he became quite intimate with the young students in painting. The decided bent of his genius induced his parents, against their wishes, to place him at the age of fourteen under Domenico Ghirlandajo, from whom he could derive little improvement except mere mechanical facility, and he soon surpassed his fellow disciples as well as his instructor.

Lorenzo the Magnificent had at that time founded an academy for the improvement of design and sculpture, and had collected in a garden at Florence a museum of antique statues, busts and bas-reliefs for the use of the students. The young Michelangelo was almost always to be found here, studying with great assiduity and enthusiasm these admirable works of antiquity; and in this school of ancient art may be said to have been developed the powers of his wonderful genius. His prog-

Michelangelo's Sketch of the Head of a Sybil

ress was soon noticed by Lorenzo, who took him under his especial protection at the age of sixteen and gave him an apartment in the Palace. This did not last, however, as Lorenzo died two years later, in 1492.

In 1508, Julius II. conceived the idea of decorating the walls and ceiling of a chapel in the Vatican, which his uncle had built from the design of Baccio Pintelli, and Michelangelo was engaged to undertake the work. This he was unwilling to do, as he had never executed any grand work in fresco, and because he was desirous of proceeding with the monument of His Holiness, for which he had made a noble design four years previous. But the Pontiff was imperative, and Angelo reluctantly began the cartoons for the ceilings of the Sistine Chapel, which he finished in 1512, in the incredibly short time of twenty months. If Michelangelo had executed no other work, this alone would have immortalized his name. It has received the universal applause of mankind, and is the most sublime monument of daring and dignified genius that the art has produced in either ancient or modern times.

It had long been disputed whether or not Michelangelo ever painted in oil; but it has been ascertained by Lanzi that the *Holy Family* in the Florentine gallery, which is the only picture by him supposed to have been painted in oil, is in reality in tempera.

The artist's chief characteristics were grandeur and sublimity. His powers were little adapted to represent the gentle and the beautiful, but whatever in nature partook of the sublime and the terrible were portrayed by him with such fidelity and grandeur as intimidates the beholder. The name of Michel-

324

angelo will be immortal as long as the peopled walls of the Sistine Chapel endure, or the mighty fabric of St. Peter's rears its proud dome above the spires of the Eternal City.

Michelangelo died on the 23rd of February, 1563, in his ninetieth year. He was buried with great pomp in the church of St. Apostoli at Rome, but afterwards, at the request of the Florentine Academy, the remains were removed to the church of Santa Croce at Florence, and were with great solemnity finally deposited in the vault by the side of the altar, called the Altare di Cavalcanti.

The studies by Raphael show his method of sketching the figure and blocking in the shapes of the shadows. There is nothing in these simple sketches by one of the greatest of masters that is not within the scope of achievement of any sincere and honest student.

By the general approbation of mankind, Raphael has been styled the prince of painters, and he is universally acknowledged to have possessed a greater combination of the higher excellencies of art than has ever fallen to the lot of any other individual. He has had severe critics, but more able defenders. It has been remarked, by Sir Joshua Reynolds among others, that the most capital frescos of Raphael in the Vatican do not at first strike the beholder with surprise, nor satisfy his expectations; but, as he begins to study them, he constantly discovers new beauties, and his admiration continues to increase with contemplation. This circumstance is accounted for by writers in various ways.

De Piles attributes it to a want of strength of coloring proper for each object, and a deficiency of chiaroscuro. George N. Taube observes that "The works of Raphael strike little at first sight, because nature is so well imitated that a spectator is no more surprised than he would be to see the object itself, which would excite no degree of surprise at all." Reynolds, after having expressed his first disappointment and subsequent admiration, says: "I am now clearly of opinion that a relish for the higher excellencies of the art is an acquired taste, which no man ever possesses without long cultivation, and great labor and attention."

These quotations express the contrariety of opinions often expressed by writers as to the merits of Raphael, especially by those superficial in art. Among other causes, doubtless, are the changes which time has wrought in depriving his frescos of their original beauty of coloring; and the fact that people who have read a great deal about any remarkable work of art or nature, frequently have their expectations so exalted that they are at first disappointed.

Raphael's greatest source of inspiration was the antique. The style of Michelangelo was not congenial to him. He had seen at least some of the latter's cartoons and pictures at Florence, though not his greatest works which were executed afterwards at Rome. Nor did Raphael study nature so attentively as some eminent masters have done, but he arrived at what nature should be. It was a maxim with him, and he taught his pupils: "We must not represent things as they are, but as they should be." Mengs says that "Raphael diligently studied the bassi-rilievi (bas-reliefs) of the arches of Titus and Constantine which were on the arch of Trajan, and adopted from them his

326

Sketch by Raphael

manner of marking the articulations of the joints, and a more simple and easier mode of expressing the contours of the fleshy parts."

Raphael, like Shakespeare, did not hesitate to appropriate anything he found in ancient or modern art that fitted his purpose; but, like the great poet, he threw around them the charm of his own incomparable genius. Michelangelo scorned to borrow anything. It is a well known fact that the beautiful arabesques with which Raphael decorated the loggie of the Vatican were copied from antiques, which he found while making excavations at the order of Leo X., though greatly improved by his own exquisite fancy. In compliance with the wishes of that pontiff, he made drawings of the ancient buildings of Rome, accompanied with descriptions, and employed the compass to ascertain the exact measurements. This valuable work was destroyed, and many of the edifices measured were destroyed in the sacking of Rome in 1527. The Abate Morelli has made public a high eulogium on this work, written by Marc' Antonio Michiel, a contemporary of Raphael's, in which it is asserted that "Raphael had drawn the ancient buildings of Rome in such a manner, and shown the proportions, form, and ornaments so correctly, that whoever had inspected them might be said to have seen ancient Rome."

Michelangelo and his party contributed not a little to the success of Raphael. As the contest between Zeuxis and Parrhasius proved beneficial to both, so the rivalry of Michelangelo and Raphael aided the fame of the former and produced the paintings in the Sistine Chapel; and at the same time contributed to the celebrity of Raphael, by producing the pictures in the Vatican, and not a few others. Michelangelo, disdaining any secondary honors, came to the combat, as it were, attended by his shield-bearer, for he made drawings in his grand style, and then gave them to Fra Sebastiano del Piombo, the scholar of Giorgione, to execute; and by this means he hoped that Raphael would never be able to rival his productions, either in design or color. Raphael stood alone, but aimed at producing works with a degree of perfection beyond the united efforts of Michelangelo and Fra Sebastiano, combining in himself a fertile imagination, ideal beauty founded on a correct imitation of the Greek style, grace, ease, amenity, and a universality of genius in every department of art. The noble determination of triumphing in such a powerful contest animated him night and day, and allowed him no respite. It also animated Raphael to surpass both his rivals and himself in every new work.

The Drawing of a Woman, by Andrea del Sarto, shows how this artist approached the study of forms by dividing them into geometric patterns. Notice the column of the neck, the oval head, and the single line for the slope of the shoulders.

Del Sarto's real name was Andrea Vannuchi, but he was called del Sarto from the occupation of his father, who was a tailor. There is considerable discrepancy as to the real merit of this painter. It has been asserted by some that, had he possessed the advantages of better early instruction, a longer residence at Rome, and more fortunate domestic relations, he would have equalled the greatest masters of the art; others declare that he was barren of invention, and that he lacked that elevation of conception, which constitutes the epic in painting as well as in poetry.

Vasari says "He was the most faultless painter of the Florentine school. He understood perfectly the principles of chiaroscuro, representing the indistinctness of objects in shadow, and painting with a sweetness truly natural. He taught how to give a perfect union to frescos, and in a great measure obviated the necessity of retouching them when dry, a circumstance which gives all his works the appearance of having been finished in one day."

Lanzi says: "He undoubtedly wanted that grandeur of conception which constitutes the highest rank in painting. Deficient in this talent, Andrea is said to have been modest, elegant, and imbued with sensibility; and it appears that he impressed this quality on nature, wherever he employed his pencil. The portico of the Nunziata, transferred by him into a gallery of inestimable value, is the fittest place to judge of his chaste outlines that procured him the surname of Andrea the Faultless. Conceptions of the graceful countenances, whose smiles remind us of the simplicity and grace of Correggio; appropriate architecture; draperies adapted to every condition, and cast with ease; popular expressions of curiosity, of astonishment, of confidence, of compassion, and of joy, never transgressing the bounds of decorum, understood at first sight, and greatly affecting the mind without agitating it, are charms that are more readily felt than expressed."

Sleeping Stable Boy by Hans Baldung is a splendid example of structural strength, showing firm anatomical lines minus

330

Andrea del Sarto's Drawing of a Woman

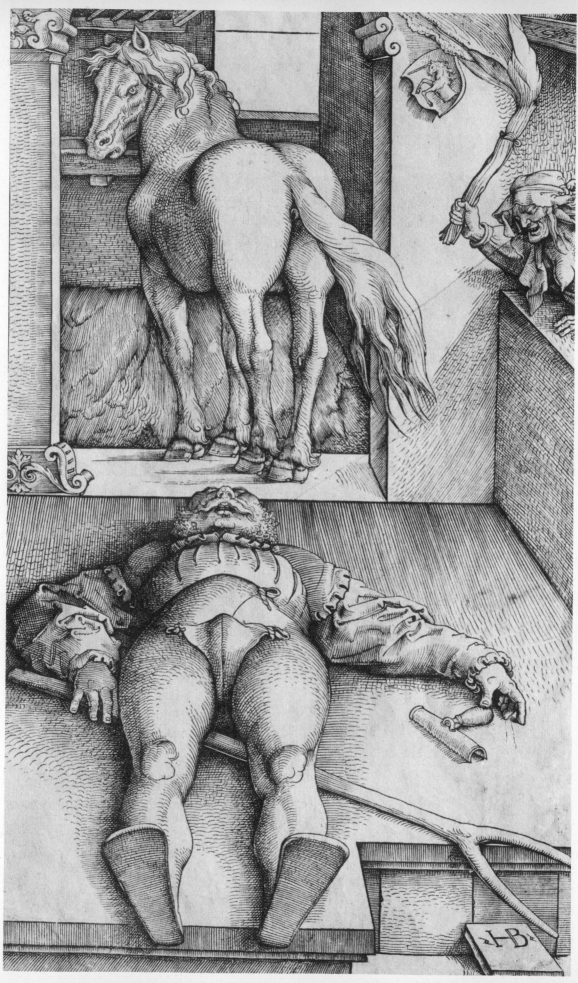

Drawing by Hans Baldung Grien

the cloying mass of unnecessary detail. The difficult perspective of horse and man attest to the vision and genius of the artist.

Baldung was a German painter and engraver, born about 1480 at Gemund, in what was then called Suabia. There are several of his paintings in the cathedral at Freiberg, in a style similar to his contemporary, Albrecht Dürer. He engraved chiefly on wood, and his blocks are executed in a free, bold style, possessing great merit.

Tintoretto, the son of a dyer, was born at Venice in 1512. From his infancy he discovered a passion for painting which exhibited itself by his sketching on walls, with a piece of charcoal, everything that struck his fancy. His father, though very poor, did not curb this propensity, but rather encouraged him, had him instructed in the rudiments of design, and at length placed him as a disciple of Titian.

Few artists have encountered such a storm of criticism as Tintoretto, and yet his best works have always extorted the admiration of his severest critics. The impetuosity of his genius and the extraordinary promptness of his hand, together with an ardent desire of embracing every opportunity of distinguishing himself, induced him to paint several large works for the convents and churches of Venice almost gratuitously, as on several occasions, the prices he received were little more than enough to defray the expense of the materials. A just idea of his merits can only be formed by contemplating his numerous pictures in the churches, convents, public edifices, and palaces at Venice. Most of his works elsewhere only exhibit

TWO BROTHERS by Tintoretto
Metropolitan Museum of Art

his infirmities. Ridolfi asserts that he finished some of his oil paintings almost as highly as miniatures, and Lanzi says that there are not wanting at Venice specimens to prove so improbable a story. Tintoretto retained his powers to a great age and died at Venice in 1594.

Peter Paul Rubens, preeminent painter, accomplished scholar and skillful diplomatist, was the son of John Rubens and Mary Pipelings, both descended from distinguished families in the city of Antwerp. His father was one of the principal magistrates of that city, at the time when the civil war obliged him to quit the Low Countries, about 1570, and seek refuge at Cologne. Rubens was born there in 1577. When Antwerp again came under the dominion of Spain, John Rubens returned to his native city and renewed the administration of his office.

Young Rubens, in his earliest years, discovered uncommon ability and vivacity of genius, literary taste, and a mild and docile disposition. His father gave him a very liberal education and, after the completion of his studies, placed him as a page with the Countess of Lalain, in order that his son might acquire graceful and accomplished manners, so important to success in a professional career.

When his father died soon afterwards, Rubens obtained his mother's permission to pursue the bent of the inclination he had discovered for painting, and she placed him under the instruction of Tobias Verhaecht, an eminent artist in landscape; but his genius inclining toward historical painting, Rubens soon left that master and entered the school of Adam Van

335

Rubens' Heads of Negroes

Oort, whose works were then in high repute. Soon again he made another change, this time studying under Venius, or van Veen, then one of the most eminent painters of the Flemish school, distinguished alike for pictorial talents, amiable and polished manners, and extensive literary attainments.

Rubens was undoubtedly one of the most original painters that ever lived, and his subjects were unlimited. He painted history, portraits, landscapes, animals, fruit and flowers, with such excellence that it is difficult to decide in which he most excelled. He possessed inexhaustible fertility of invention, never copying himself or any other master, in so many and varied productions.

Rubens did not, like Raphael, possess that mild inspiration of sentiment which manifests itself in dignified and noble, or graceful and beautiful forms, but he was animated with a poetic fire that displays itself in surprising or astonishing effects.

The powers of his imagination were so abundant that his most extensive compositions seem to have been produced without effort, and creation appears an operation of his will. This is evident from his admirable productions in the Luxembourg, and many other works too well known to need description. He is generally allowed to have carried coloring to its highest excellence; his groups are disposed with such skill as to conduct the eye of the observer at once to the principal object. His draperies are simple, broad and grand; his carnations have the appearance of nature and the warmth of life. It cannot be denied that he preferred brilliancy of effect to beauty of form, and frequently sacrificed correctness of design to the magic of coloring, probably from his impetuosity of conception and rapidity of execution.

Genius is always bold and daring, and while it commands attention and admiration, is sure to provoke criticism. The styles of the three greatest painters, Michelangelo, Raphael and Rubens, were entirely different, and it is very certain that, had they adopted any other, they never would have reached the excellence and renown which they achieved.

In this Gallery you will find a drawing of a woman's head by Rubens. It is very expressive, shaded lightly and with subtlety. The construction of the mouth, nose and eyes are nicely defined for study.

Drawing of a Woman's Head by Rubens

The next drawing is particularly interesting because Vandyck was celebrated for his portraits of mounted men. The horse sketch, while crude, nevertheless has beautiful swing and verve.

Sir Anthony Vandyck was born at Antwerp in 1599. His father was a glass-painter of Bois-le-Duc, in good circumstances, and gave him his early instruction in drawing. He was also instructed by his mother, who painted landscapes and who was very skillful in embroidery. He studied afterwards under Henry Van Balen and made rapid progress in the art; but, attracted by the fame of Rubens, he entered the school of that master, and showed so much ability as to be soon entrusted with the execution of some of his instructor's designs. Some writers assert that Rubens became jealous of Vandyck's growing excellence, and therefore advised him to devote himself to portrait painting; assigning the following anecdote as the immediate cause of this jealousy.

During the short absences of Rubens from his house, for the purpose of recreation, his disciples frequently obtained access to his studio, by means of bribing an old servant who kept the keys; and on one of these occasions, while they were all pressing forward eagerly to view the great picture of the *Descent from the Cross* (although later investigations concerning dates seem to indicate that it was some other picture), Diepenbeck accidentally fell against the canvas, effacing the face of the Virgin and the Magdalen's arm, which had just been finished and were not yet dry. Fearful of expulsion from the school, the terrified students chose Vandyck to restore the work, and he completed it the same day with such success that

Rubens did not at first perceive the change, and afterwards concluded not to alter it. Walpole entertains a different and more rational view respecting Rubens' supposed jealousy; he thought that Vandyck felt the hopelessness of surpassing his master in historical painting, and therefore resolved to devote himself to portraiture.

Although Vandyck acquired his great fame in portraits, he painted also many historical pieces, and he never at any time ceased operating in this department. Inferior to Rubens in boldness of conception and fertility of invention, he never could have equalled him in historical painting; but his compositions are arranged with judgment and propriety; he surpassed Rubens in correctness of design, the delicate expression of his heads, and the truth, purity, and harmony of his coloring.

Paul van Rhyn Rembrandt was one of the most notable painters and engravers of the Dutch school. He was the son of a miller, and was born in 1606 at a small village on the banks of the Rhine. He was called Rembrandt van Rhyn, though his family name was Gerretz. He entered the school of Jacob van Zwaanenberg at Amsterdam, where he continued for three years. Having learned all that instructor was able to impart, he next studied for about six months with Peter Lastmann, and afterwards for a short time with Jacob Pinas, from whom it is said he acquired that taste for strong contrasts of light and shadow for which his works are so remarkable. He was, however, more indebted for his best improvement to the vivacity of his own genius and an attentive study of nature,

Drawing by Vandyck

than to any information that he derived from his instructors.

Rembrandt had already brought both the arts of painting and engraving to very great perfection (in his own way), when a slight incident led him to fame and fortune. He was induced by a friend to take one of his choicest pictures to a picture-dealer at the Hague, who, being charmed with the performance, instantly gave him a hundred florins for it, and treated him with great respect. This occurrence served to convince the public of his merit, and contributed to make the artist sensible of his own abilities.

Rembrandt holds a distinguished rank among the engravers of his country; he established a more important epoch in this art than any other master. He was indebted entirely to his own genius for the invention of a process which has thrown an indescribable charm over his plates. They are partly etched, frequently much assisted by the drypoint, and occasionally, though rarely, finished with the graver; evincing the most extraordinary facility of the hand, and displaying the most consummate knowledge of the effects of light and shadow. His free and playful point sports in picturesque disorder, producing the most surprising and enchanting effects, as of by accident; yet an examination will show that his motions are always regulated by a profound knowledge of the principles of light and shadow. His most admirable productions in both arts are his portraits, which are executed with unexampled expression and skill.

The heads reproduced in this Gallery are drawn in such a way as to make the comparatively few lines combine with the background and light areas with the implication of great de-

342

Etchings by Rembrandt

tail. The heads of the old men are wonderful studies in elimination.

Franz Hals, who painted the *Bohemian Girl,* was born at Mechlin in 1584, and died in 1666. He was a disciple of Karel van Mander. He was a contemporary and friend of Vandyck, and in their particular branch of the art of painting he has been surpassed by none of the artists of his country, except by the latter. His coloring is chaste, but vigorous, and his heads are full of life and character.

It is said that Vandyck invited him to accompany him to

BOHEMIAN GIRL by Franz Hals

England, where his talents would be properly rewarded; and that great painter was of the opinion that no Flemish artist would have equalled Hals, had he given more tenderness to his coloring. He painted, with remarkable accuracy and vigor, a large picture containing the portraits of the members of the Company of Archers at Delft for their hall.

Francois Boucher's soft and delicate nudes are not as boneless as they appear to be at first glance. Partially close your eyes when you look at his *Cupid Sporting,* and you will see the fine, divided planes and the feeling of strong structure underneath.

Boucher was a Parisian painter and engraver who was born in 1704, died in 1768. He studied under Francois Le Moine,

CUPID SPORTING. By Francois Boucher

was appointed court painter, and was favored with the patronage of the great. Few painters have enjoyed in their lifetime the flattering encouragement and great reputation of Boucher; and perhaps never was there one who enjoyed these advantages with less real claim to them. He was a perfect master of the mechanism of the art, and deserves great credit for that; but he openly set at naught the truly beautiful, and corrupted the public taste. He succeeded best in pastoral subjects, though they are not equal to those of Watteau.

Jean Baptiste Greuze, a French painter of fancy subjects and conversation pieces, was born at Tournus in 1726. He early manifested a strong inclination for design, in which he was violently opposed by his father; but happening to attract the notice of Grandon, a portrait painter of Lyons, he was taken to his school, where he soon made rapid progress. He afterwards went to Paris and produced his celebrated picture of the *Father explaining the Scriptures to his Children,* which at once established his reputation, and he was soon extensively employed.

His works are highly valued for their exquisite coloring, particularly in his carnations; and for the fine models of his heads and countenances. His pictures are full of life and sensibility, and his heads of young girls possess a charming innocence and simplicity that deserves the highest praise. In the composition shown here, the group is made dynamic by the geometric forms of his figures and the objects around them. Notice how the clothing of the two women has been worked out into large forms.

Drawing by Jean Baptiste Greuze

William Blake's *When the Morning Stars Sang Together* was included in this collection to show the architectural structure of the row of figures at the top of the composition. His conventionalized figures fitted admirably into his formally designed compositions. Blake was born in 1757, and died in 1828. He was apprenticed to Basire, the engraver. His genius was undoubted, but his mind was unbalanced. In some of his illustrations we are sometimes surprised by the invention and sublimity displayed by the artist; while at others, his extravagant flights invoke our admiration. He is perhaps better known today for his poetry, but he gained little encouragement during his lifetime, and died in poverty.

Daumier's compositions show his specialty of expressing strong emotions in his characters. He could convey the essence of despair, weariness or pain in one sweep of his uncompromisingly direct brush. Examine his *Third Class Railway Carriage*. Without bothering about muscle movements and bone protuberances, he puts enormous power and pathos into the hands of his peasants.

The French nineteenth century painter, La Lyre, has given us a group of strong studies. Fine division of the forms of light and shade, and a powerful sweep of line are achieved with an economy of effort. The medium used is charcoal. In the last drawing of this Gallery, La Lyre has sketched his figures directly and strongly in a rough design for a mural. The area is divided into squares for the purpose of keeping the same proportion when blocking the enlarged mural design.

WHEN THE MORNING STARS SANG TOGETHER by William Blake.
Metropolitan Museum of Art, New York

THIRD CLASS RAILWAY CARRIAGE by Daumier

First in a series of eight charcoal sketches by La
Lyre. The others appear on the following pages.

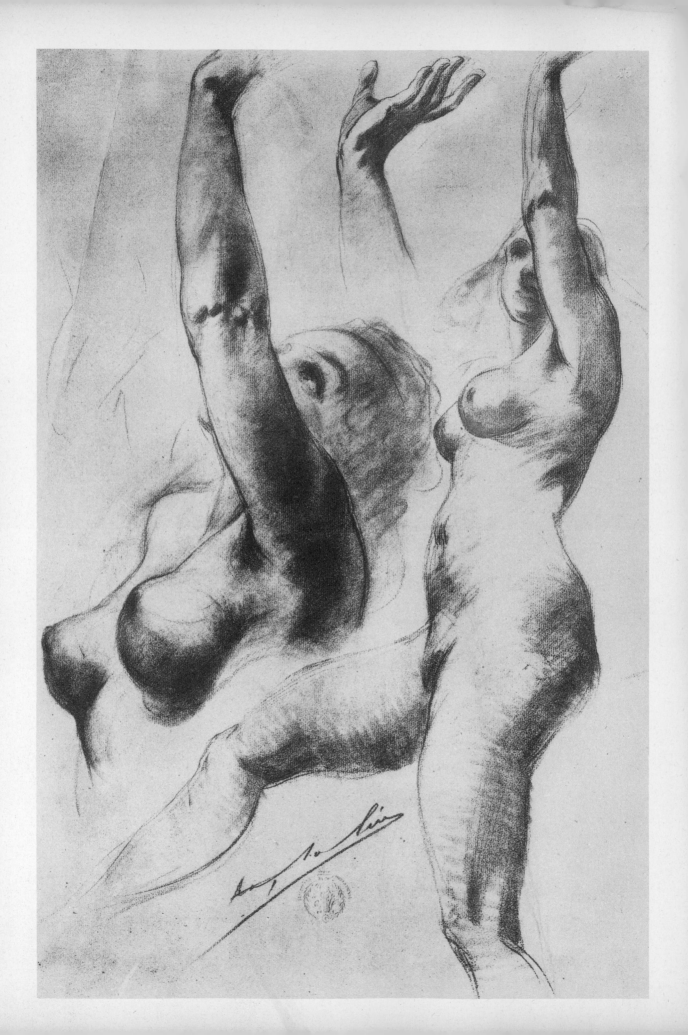

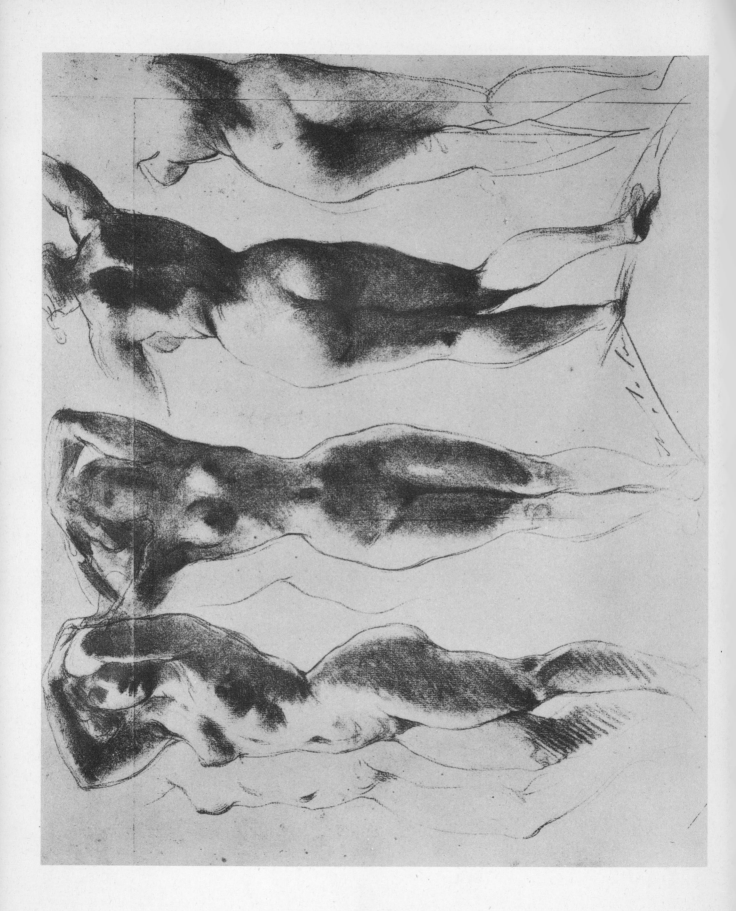

Five Hundred Years *of* Illustration

*FROM ALBRECHT DÜRER
TO ROCKWELL KENT*

By Howard Simon

HERE is an important work by Howard Simon, one of our leading contemporary artists, who is qualified to trace the development of book illustration from the invention of printing in the Fifteenth Century to the present day.

Every illustrator of importance—Durer, Hogarth, Rowlandson, Goya, Blake, Daumier, Cruikshank, Kent, Artzybasheff, Claire Leighton, etc.—is included in this five century survey which consists of a textual account of the life and period of these great artists and over 600 accurate reproductions of their best works. Among these will be found many prints that are unavailable in any book.

This magnificent edition is a prized volume for the collector . . . an invaluable reference work for the artist . . . a treasured possession for all who interest themselves in the charm and seriousness of art.

Price $2.50

Attractively printed and handsomely bound.
Get a copy from your book-seller; if he
cannot supply you, send your order direct to

ILLUSTRATED EDITIONS COMPANY

220 FOURTH AVENUE   NEW YORK

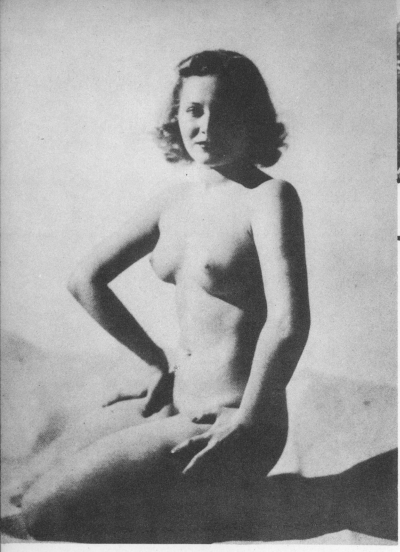

Much of the beauty of the female form arises from the relation of the breasts to other parts of the body. The breasts parallel the shoulders. They are halfway between shoulders and navel, circle around from the median line of the chest until the outer curves rest on the inner arm, and face away from each other at a right angle; as the little elevation at the tip of each breast indicates.

This splendid volume is intended primarily as an aid for the art student and instructor. It is a well-known fact that no artist can attain any degree of excellence in his chosen field unless he has devoted a certain amount of time to drawing from "life" or the nude. And it is equally true that, save for the largest cities, American communities offer the embryo artist very few facilities for completing this extremely important phase of his work. It is to fill this void that *Body in Art* is now offered to the American public, and collaborating in its production were two of the most eminent authorities in their respective professions: Alexander Paal and Arthur Zaidenberg.

Size 9⅞ by 12⅞

Body in Art brings to you the finest "life" class obtainable. Over eighty poses—including front, side, back views and mixed figures—give the student a widely diversified range of study. Of the utmost importance are the dozens of studies selected by Arthur Zaidenberg, author of *Anyone Can Draw* and art instructor at *New York University*. He has drawn and analyzed each study, showing step by step the important details, from a few simple lines to the completed figure. The models, too, have been selected with great care, and are far superior in form and symmetry to those ordinarily seen at the average "life" class. Among them are many who have won international fame and recognition for their beauty and grace.

ILLUSTRATED EDITIONS COMPANY

220 Fourth Avenue   New York

This charming seated figure enables the sincere artist to discover the structural basis of beauty. Since all the ribs are firmly attached to the spine and turn with it, they must swing the entire trunk as a unit. However, because the shoulders are not attached to the spine or ribs they have free movement. The breasts also are not connected to the skeletal frame, and show their elasticity by changing shape as the body alters position.

To recapture the particular artistic effect of this lovely photograph, regard the long full sweep from the neck, around the back and hips, to the bent knee. The body is made to appear at ease by the natural support of outstretched leg and arm. See also how the line of the arm, which at first parallels the sweep of the back, interrupts the long curve, and in so doing produces a pleasant feeling of static beauty.

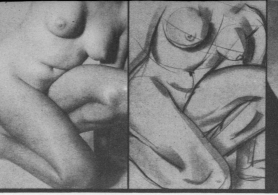

This photograph provides a splendid and interesting study in perspective in its relation to the female figure. By actual measurement the knees and thighs are never as large as the torso. But because they are so much closer to the eye they must appear larger, and the senses accept that enlargement as realistic. Note, too, how the laws of perspective enlarge the breasts as they reach forward from the body.

Most persons lack ability to see the full beauty of a camera portrait. They see too much detail, yet fail to grasp the special charm of large masses separated—yet drawn together—by shadows. Examine this photograph and sketch to understand that point. See how unimportant details may be eliminated without loss of pictorial value, while major features are thrown into relief that heighten the effect of charming grace.

Body in Art

BY ALEXANDER PAAL

These photographs must be seen in their full-page size in order to be fully appreciated. The arrangement of poses and the photography has been done by Alexander Paal, in whose hands the camera becomes a precision instrument rendering true perfection in every detail. A past master in the use of lighting effects and arrangements, Paal has arranged many of his subjects so that the essentials of form and balance can readily be grasped by the novice. Other poses have been made more complex so that as the student advances he will find full play for his talent. Those who have had basic training in drawing from life will also find in such pictures ample scope for their ability and an inexpensive means of continuing their study.

INDIVIDUALLY BOXED—$2.75

Study how this beautifully posed woman illustrates the principle of balance. The body bends forward from the waist. So, while the left leg supports the greater part of the weight, the right leg is thrust forward and to the side to provide another point of balance. In your preliminary outline, this must be provided for by drawing the "line of balance" from the left foot through the center of the body; which is also the center of weight.

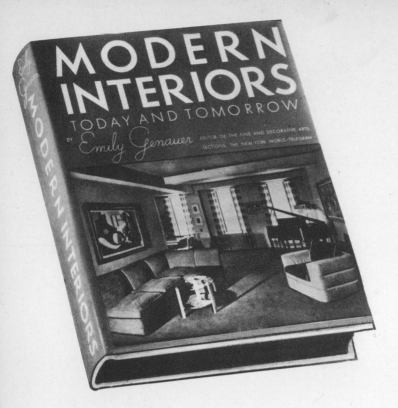

4)(H) 234
       234
       204